"John Lodal's candi‹ ing experience of gri lost a beloved person. ....p........, ...r those left-brain dominant folks who hope to think their way out of grief. As a pastor for many years who has walked beside grieving people, I know this book will be helpful to many and will offer an invitation to awaken the whole of one's self to experience the depth of feelings and the breadth of blessings that accompany loss."

~Reverend Barbara Nixon,
Spiritual Direction/Theological Reflection
"Interfaith Voices," Albany/ Corvallis Newspapers

"Join John Lodal on a journey from the logic of the mind to the wisdom of the heart and watch as he integrates both as he navigated his own cancer, that of his beloved wife, and the profound grief of her death. How do we redefine ourselves during traumatic change? How does a 'human doing' become a 'human being' when the biggest accomplishment is getting through the day? John asks and answers these questions with a vulnerability, transparency, and hope that inspires."

~Maureen O'Toole, Cancer Survivor
Retired US Army Officer, Author, Community Leader

"John crafts a beautiful picture of his love of wife and life. He reveals his maelstrom of grief then brings the reader on his discovery, recovery, and ongoing remapping of his heart and happiness. To the universal experience of loss, John brings light and a fresh perspective: a pathway for grief and growth to forge partnership as a key to swing open doors to life after loss. He pens with hope and gratitude."

~Maril McCord – MPT, Boise, Idaho

"As a Grief Recovery Specialist, I regularly meet people who have a very hard time accessing, exploring, and healing their feelings that are often related to a deep loss. My experience has been that these individuals are often men who, like John, are far more comfortable in their left brain. I recommend this book to all, right- or left-brained, who struggle to know and understand their feelings. John's personal story of integrating his head and heart will hold up a mirror for others who want to do the same."

~Carol Betts, M.S., Life Coach and
Advanced Grief Recovery Specialist

"Grief will invade your life, and you will not get a vote on the fact that it's arrived. Despite the near universality of losing those we love most, few of us are well-equipped to deal with our grief. This moving account of the author's journey from a devastating loss to a place of gratitude provides valuable lessons for all who experience loss."

~Joel Horton, Former Idaho Supreme Court Justice

"This book is about the journey of grief through the eyes of an engineer. Used to being able to figure things logically, he realized that grief has no logic. By way of self-observation, John ascertained the tools needed to move forward: faith, family, and friends. John affirms that GriefShare helped on his journey; he began to find peace once he discovered how to share his grief."

~Dawn Veenstra

"As a fellow left-brained engineer who's spent a lifetime deploying the cudgel of logic and analysis to fix my problems, I'm humbled and moved by John's insights and prescriptions for navigating the path of grief that we'll all eventually travel. This book is not for the timid—it's in your face—but provides an uplifting (and often humorous) roadmap for embracing our other (right brain) side to really feel; to grapple with fear and anger and guilt and separation; and the quixotic quest for the 'meaning of meaning' that accompanies us along this journey. One doesn't need to be spiritually inclined (or an engineer!) to embrace *A Right Brain Awakening*, but being open, honest, and inquisitive sure helps. I have no doubt that many, many folks will find this work an invaluable ally when the inevitable, thornier parts of Life show up."

~Steve Banick, Author of *Accidental Enlightenment*

"I got to know John and Pam through Rotary. I started out as spectator of their journeys with cancer. The more I got to understand how John's engineering brain processed the events as Pam's cancer progressed and she was called home, I was able to share with John a couple of books on working through grief. He and I had several conversations regarding his new journey. *A Right Brain Awakening* is an outpouring of raw feelings and a true-life reemergence of the new John.

I believe anyone who has suffered a loss and is having a tough time processing and trying to figure out how to move forward will benefit from the lessons John learned and has shared. I must warn you to keep a tissue close by during some parts of the book. Thank you, John, for sharing and giving me some insights on how to deal with such a personal loss.

~Steve Gage, Rotary Club of Boise Sunrise

"John courageously abandons his comfort zone, a calculated and systematic approach to the world, and takes us on his deeply personal journey through the uncharted wilderness of grief and loss. What a beautiful testament to the love that John and Pam shared, to the painful, relatable discoveries of grief, and to the sacred mystery of life."

~Jerri Walker, M.A., Licensed Professional Counselor

"John Lodal, a left-brained engineer, had to learn how to let his right brain help him find his way through grief. He shares about taking care of his wife as she was dying from cancer and how a grief counselor helped him face and talk about his trauma. He offers concrete suggestions for how men can understand their emotions. His book will appeal to widowers and those who are trying to help them. We need more men to write about grief from their perspective."

~Mark Liebenow,
Author of www.widowersgrief.blogspot.com

"John's deeply honest, courageous, personal story of how he transformed the searing pain of losing his wonderful wife into a deep commitment to grow and to help others struggling with deep loss will resonate with and help many left-brained people. As another engineer who worked with John and also lost a spouse, I found his grappling with emotional literacy and digging into the deepest tenets of his spiritual tradition to be helpful approaches for us left-brained folks. His recommended reading list is also right on. John's book is a gift to the world and especially us nerds!"

~Lisa Hecht, Career Coach,
Retired Program Manager and Electrical Engineer

A
Right Brain
Awakening

A
Right Brain
Awakening

WHAT GRIEF TAUGHT
A HEARTBROKEN ENGINEER

John Lodal

Stonebrook Publishing
Saint Louis, Missouri

A STONEBROOK PUBLISHING BOOK

©2022 John Lodal

Library of Congress Control Number: 2022918237

Paperback ISBN: 978-1-955711-20-3

eBook ISBN: 978-1-955711-21-0

www.stonebrookpublishing.net

PRINTED IN THE UNITED STATES OF AMERICA

*This book is dedicated to
my wife, Pam. I will forever be
grateful for the great love that
I was allowed to experience
when she chose me to
be her husband.
Gotemdo, Paru.*

CONTENTS

PREFACE

This book was birthed from the pain of losing my wife, Pam, to cancer on Halloween in 2019.

None of us is going to get off this globe alive, and most of us will experience some type of searing grief. The fact that there is grief in all our lives made this writing project a priority for me because I think I have a unique point of view as a full-on, Type-A, left brain engineer who was thrust upon this journey. There don't seem to be many books written from this left-brain point of view. Thus, this tome.

My left brain was so dominant (and my right brain so dormant) that when my grief counselor asked for my reaction to a word cloud of "feelings-related" words, I was slightly embarrassed to admit I'd never used these words to describe myself—words like *resentful, empowered, defiant, guilty, angry, hurt,* and *sad.* All words that are part of our normal, human emotional makeup.

But as I processed my wife's death and its aftermath, I was assaulted by such feelings. For example, the word *resentful.* This was an emotion that I thought I'd removed from my life, but it returned with a punch after Pam died. Words like *hurt* or *anxious* or *jealous* now had to be confronted. I was alone and without the love of my life. I was way off balance and felt like no one understood the persistent weight of my new status as a widower.

How could this have happened? was a question that entered my mind time and time again. All my planning and dreaming of the future meant nothing now that Pam was gone. And I didn't have the tools to deal with these new feelings. Other emotions, like *guilty, angry, hurt,* and *sad,* now rushed forward. I was adrift and this word cloud brought many of my new challenges into sharper focus. My right brain was going to have to step up to guide me in what was next, but it was underdeveloped and needed to be sharpened.

Pam fought a courageous and fierce battle with head and neck cancer until it got the upper hand in late 2019. She and I were—at different times—both diagnosed with identical cancer (left base of tongue), which was ultimately attributed to HPV, Human Papilloma Virus. The doctors couldn't explain why, after decades of fidelity, the virus expressed itself in each of us. She went three rounds with it, and during the second round, she had a laryngectomy after the cancer returned to her epiglottis. So, we saw the end coming, and this gave us at least two years, clearly knowing that our time together was finite. I believe that we pressed the let's-live-this-life-fully pedal down hard in those last few years. Although it took time for me to gain this perspective, I now know that time was a real blessing.

Grief will invade your life, and you will not get a vote on the fact that it's arrived. But there are effective ways to push back on this rather grim forecast. Some of my left-brain—problem-solving, engineering—mental wiring served me well. Seeing what was really going on and where it was leading allowed me to endure this process with a minimum of guilt or *what if...* musings. But there are other significant things I learned and changes I went through as my right brain awakened—and I didn't see them coming. These evolutions of John are what have made me the man I am today, a much different man than I was before I lost my wife. Those changes continue to occur, and I'm doing my best to pay attention with my eyes, ears, and heart wide open.

Before this journey, when my right brain gradually awakened, several friends had described me as a *human-doing* rather than a *human being*. I accept that description as being accurate. I'll also assert that there's noticeable progress toward the human-*being* evolution apparent in me now. In fact, my willingness to write this book is one of the manifestations of my right brain coming online in a more conscious manner.

In this book, I tell stories about how I moved forward after the train wreck of Pam's death. That collection of stories and epiphanies can veer into dark spaces and make this a heavy read. But I want to ensure that you get to know the extraordinary person Pam was and explore some of the curious humor that accompanied my journey. With this in mind, I'll share some stories about my wife that will allow you to get to know her better. These first two deal with the immediate aftermath of her laryngectomy surgery in February 2017.

Our son, Geoff, and I were allowed to visit Pam in her ICU room at Huntsman Cancer Institute in Salt Lake City (SLC) after not seeing her for fourteen hours during her laryngectomy on February 14, 2017. Numerous doctors and nurses were getting her installed and set up, and she was still sleepy after this major surgery. It was great to see her, and she was glad to see these two important men in her life.

I joked and said, "She looks pretty beat up."

And then Geoff directed my gaze at her right hand. "Dad, do you see how Mom responded to your last comment?"

She was smiling and playfully flipping me off with her middle finger. I didn't think I could laugh on this challenging day, but Pam got me going.

I looked at her and lovingly said, "Well played, my dear."

I knew we were going to be OK even though we had a long journey in front of us. She had accepted her new reality with some dark humor and was letting me know that it was time for me to do the same.

A few months later, when the initial healing had occurred, it was time to embrace a milestone moment on that journey of healing. It demonstrates, yet again, how well she appeared to accept our new reality and was a direct reference to how she would sound with her new voice.

After Pam's laryngectomy, I received detailed care instructions from her surgeons at Huntsman. Drs. Monroe and Buchmann told me, "John, it's important that Pam not use her voice for at least a month. Work with your SLP (Speech and Language Pathologist) to dial in exactly when might be a good time to give her new voice a try."

We followed that guidance rigorously, and she used a Boogie Board (a reusable and electronically erasable writing tablet) effectively to communicate with me and others. I was looking forward to hearing her voice again as the one-month anniversary approached. Along the way, I decided to grow a Fu Manchu mustache. Pam was not fond of this facial hair, but I turned it into something that I felt would benefit both of us.

I told her, "I'll shave it off when you tell me—verbally—to do it."

We went to the appointment at Saint Luke's Speech Therapy, and Karen, her SLP, worked with her to get everything ready for the first trial of her new voice. This was a highly emotional moment for us.

When everything was ready, Karen asked Pam, "Please say your name."

And I heard that new voice for the first time. I was so moved that I had to sit down and process this emotionally intense milestone moment. While I was taking my seat, I heard the second thing that she chose to say.

Pam told me, "You need to go home and shave." I could no longer hold back the tears. I shaved an hour later.

THIS IS NOT AN EASY STORY TO TELL, but I want to share what I've learned. I started this journey as a left-brain, problem-solving engineer who, as my default, shuffled deep emotions and powerful feelings off to the side. Then a bomb went off in my life, and I was forced to recognize that *I would have to change* if I was going to deal with these new feelings in a meaningful way.

I believe there are others who are in that same situation. I read many books to help soothe my pain, but I never found a single one that started with the point of view of a left-brain-dominant, right-brain-challenged individual. I hope this book can fill that gap and offer you ideas about how to allow grief to teach your broken heart.

OUR STORY

P art of my training as an engineer at Hewlett Packard (HP), a multinational information technology firm in Boise, Idaho, was to communicate clearly and succinctly. The clear part was easy; the succinct part was more challenging. When I gave status updates to my management at HP, I was encouraged to get to the point quickly—tell them the conclusion right away, explain how I came to that conclusion, and then open it up for questions and challenges from my audience.

With that training in mind, it seems appropriate to describe what happened before and during the process of losing Pam to this heartless disease of cancer. My left-brain training was only partially appropriate for this situation. I always wanted to fix any issues for my wife or children because that type of behavior was valued and rewarded at HP. Define the issue, kick around ideas about how to understand its root causes, run some experiments to see if these hypotheses were on target, and then fix the issue in the most expedient, corrective manner possible. During both our battles with cancer, this approach helped a lot. But when we entered hospice during the last six weeks of Pam's life, it was not effective at all. For that, I needed new skills that were rooted in faith and grounded in good listening skills. I'd never been known for being a good listener.

I was diagnosed with head and neck cancer myself in September 2012, and it was a tremendous shock. I'd been on my way to a big band rehearsal when I got the call from my primary care doctor.

"John, I'm afraid I have bad news," he said. "I reviewed your lab reports, and there's active cancer in your neck."

Looking back, I realize that my brain fuzzed out significantly, and this was one of those times when certain mental circuit breakers in my brain blew open so I could continue functioning. I believe that these circuit breakers are part of our psychological makeup, and they switch to an open status when we're confronted with overwhelming grief or sadness.

That initial diagnosis came from a fine-needle aspiration of new and troublesome lumps in my neck. But it also revealed a curiosity—these cancerous cells originated somewhere else in my body. Because my treatment, Intense Modulated Radiation Therapy (IMRT), caused significant collateral damage to all tissue along the lines of the radiation beam, it was critical that we find the primary tumor. In the days after the diagnosis, I had two CT scans and one PET scan to pinpoint the exact location of my primary tumor. But those three scans didn't find the source of my tumor, and I was scheduled for surgery in early October.

The surgery opened the left side of my neck, and they found the tumor at the left base of my tongue. A round two-centimeter collection of squamous non-small-cell cancer cells was growing deep down into my neck. Numerous lymph nodes and one sub-mandibular gland were removed. Since they couldn't remove the primary tumor because that would mean I'd lose my tongue, the key was to find it, so they could radiate it.

Now the radiation oncologist knew where to aim the ray guns. I was to get 100 percent of my lifetime dose of radiation on that spot, with lower amounts around the tumor. Therefore, they used the intensity modulated type of radiation. During the therapy, they bolted me down to a table and shot at the tumor from nine different angles. The machine rotated around my head, and I felt absolutely nothing during each of these thirty-five sessions, five mornings a week for seven weeks. I could hear the shutters in the radiation machine (depleted uranium blocks moving in a linear fashion to deliver the precise dosage to each part of my neck), and in about five or ten minutes, the session was complete.

The physical decline from the cumulative effects of radiation didn't appear until the third week. Mouth sores, lack of appetite (which ultimately required a feeding tube), and a general malaise surfaced as the treatment took a physical toll on my health. By the end of it all, I'd lost my voice, my sense of taste, and forty pounds—20 percent of my body weight.

I also received a weekly dose of chemotherapy using Cisplatin to combat any cancerous cells that may have escaped the ray guns and moved to other parts of my body. It was a brutal therapy regimen, and my team at St. Luke's Mountain States Tumor Institute (MSTI) in Idaho claimed that head and neck therapy was among the nastiest to endure. I agreed. I was totally beat up by late December 2012, when active therapy was complete.

I was declared cancer-free in February 2013, and the feeding tube was removed soon after. My voice came back, but it was markedly different from before, lower and raspier. My sense of taste also returned, but certain things never tasted the same again. My weight stayed down for about a year. The radiobiology that killed the targeted cancer cells had significantly revved up my metabolism, and I was able to eat like a horse for those twelve months without putting on any weight.

I had significant permanent damage to my salivary glands, so I became a regular gum chewer, as long as that gum was sweetened by Sorbitol. Radiation patients like me can experience devastating dental damage due to the lack of salivary action, so I also used dental trays and fluoride treatments to prevent tooth damage. But I was alive and able to quietly appreciate how tough I'd been to endure those sledgehammer treatments.

And then we had to do it all again with Pam.

In the summer of 2015, Pam was diagnosed with the exact same cancer on the left base of her tongue. We were stunned. We now swapped the role of patient and caregiver, having gone through this brutal therapy regimen a few years earlier. She was tough and probably stronger in resolve than I was during this process. In addition to the problems I had, the chemo caused her significant tinnitus, which was a constant ringing in her ears. We hunkered down again, and Pam dealt with her own collection of thirty-five therapy sessions with the ray gun.

She actively engaged in the rehab process, much like I had. We had each gone toe-to-toe with the beast and emerged cancer free. It was time to reclaim our lives and ponder the perspective that was associated with being cancer *survivors*. We could now both walk in the American Cancer Society's Relay for Life wearing purple shirts and could share dark humor stories of treatment and side effects with other survivors. We had prevailed, and we had intimate knowledge of each other's journey.

But in late 2016, our stories diverged. During one of her follow-up visits with our head and neck surgeon, the results indicated a reoccurrence of her cancer. This was a dark time because active therapy was to be administered by a team of specialists at Huntsman Cancer Institute (HCI) in Salt Lake City. Unfortunately, we had to wait six long weeks to see these specialists, which was emotionally agonizing.

When we finally met with this impressive team at HCI, the news was hard to bear. The returning cancer had spread to Pam's epiglottis, a critical flap of cartilage near the base of the tongue. The mechanical functioning of the throat is a beautiful and complex thing to witness. The key component is the epiglottis, which acts like a well-designed valve to ensure that food doesn't enter the lungs (a process known as aspirating) while also enabling breathing and speech. Pam's epiglottis would have to be removed, which would radically change her voice and move her breathing to a new stoma, an opening into the trachea on her neck. She was going to become a laryngectomee, which meant she would forever be a neck breather. The sole purpose of her mouth would now be to ingest food and fluids, as well as a new form of speech called an *esophageal voice*. The drive back from Salt Lake City to Boise was a very quiet one as we each pondered the major changes that would take place on Valentine's Day 2017.

The laryngectomy surgery took almost twelve hours and involved two extremely skilled surgeons. The first removed the cancer and the related tissue that would render Pam cancer free. The second surgeon put her back together again. The complexity of this reassembly process was mind-blowing. Pam was in the Intensive Care Unit at HCI for three days and then in the post-surgical ward for another four days. I will always be amazed at how quickly she made this initial recovery. We'd been told to expect a hospital stay of six to eight weeks, but we were headed home to Boise in seven days. Wow! This was a true testament to Pam's inner strength.

Being her caregiver involved an enormous number of tasks to properly support her needs for nutrition, pain management, wound management, and general rehab. After she left the HCI surgical theater, I never heard her original voice again. In fact, to support her healing, she was not allowed to exercise her voice at all for more than a month. Our grandchildren helped us discover an electronically erasable device called a Boogie Board, and she used one to communicate during and after that period of silence.

Hearing Pam speak again at the Speech Pathology Department at Saint Luke's was a high point. She sounded very different, but I had so missed hearing her that I needed to sit and gather my emotions for a few minutes. She had beaten the beast again! We knew that she'd been given another chance and that there was no holding back in terms of living our best lives. We could watch our grandchildren grow up. We could take some of the big trips that we'd dreamed about. Most importantly, we still had each other.

Soon, we discovered the Caring Bridge website, an online forum for patients who want to share the details of their journey with friends and loved ones in a blog format. My initial goal was to tell the stories of Pam's progress in one central place rather than having to repeat the details over and over for friends and family. Pam agreed this was a sound approach, and so I dusted off my writing skills. The technical part of these posts was simple. I'd been doing my fair share of technical writing at HP, so I knew how to get to the point and communicate the information in an understandable manner. But other aspects of our health adventure started to work their way into my posts. Deep emotions and revelations emerged as we journeyed into new territory, and I had to sit with these new feelings for a bit to decide exactly how to share them. My posts addressed the nuts and bolts of Pam's health, as well as her emotions and psyche—and my thoughts and feelings as her caregiver.

Pam also began making Caring Bridge posts. She found her writer's voice and posted about how she was doing and what she felt. Now we had two different voices/authors represented in one Caring Bridge account. Our stories resonated with readers and evoked heartfelt replies. The tangible support from this blog significantly lifted our spirits. It was fundamentally therapeutic for both of us, individually and as a couple. We began to see the true nature of what Caring Bridge could do for us and our followers beyond simply sharing the medical details of Pam's journey.

Here is some of what Pam wrote:

—January 30, 2017

By now you have most likely heard that my cancer has returned. At this point, the best (only) treatment option to completely get rid of the cancer is to have a laryngectomy. This has been scheduled for February 14th at Huntsman Cancer Institute in Salt Lake City. What a way to celebrate Valentine's Day! But a friend of mine said, "Bummer to have surgery on that day but a great day to give the gift of new health." Thank you for that positive outlook, Jenny!

This CaringBridge site will let us keep you updated on my progress. For about two weeks after surgery, I will be limited to written, non-verbal, or pre-recorded communication. (Yes, that will be difficult for me!) After that I will work with the wonderful SLPs (Speech Language Pathologists) at St. Luke's here in Boise to learn how to use a voice prosthesis.

Yes, I'm a little sad and a little scared, but a LOT hopeful. Most importantly, I am grateful for my wonderful support network—family, friends, and, most of all, my rock, John.

—February 7, 2017

I'm a big fan of hugs, and I've been getting a lot of them recently. I hope that doesn't change. I remember that it was sometimes awkward to receive a hug when I was going through my radiation/chemotherapy due to having a port and a feeding tube. I hope that having a stoma doesn't keep you from giving me a hug.

It is now one week until my surgery, and I've been doing a lot of reading on the internet and in books about what's ahead. I have mixed feelings about calling myself a "laryngectomee" because I don't want this procedure to define who I am. I want people to look at and see ME— not just the hole in my neck. I want people to focus on WHAT I am saying and not just the way the words sound. I have read stories from people who hide their stomas with scarves and accessories and from those who want to show off their stoma like a badge of honor. I wonder where I'll fall into that spectrum.

Thank you all for your words of encouragement, your prayers, and your hugs! I am so grateful to have such love and support from family and friends!

Pam

—February 13, 2017

This is Pam again. John will be writing the next few journal entries as I start my healing and rehab.

It's been a great day here in Salt Lake City. We met with my second surgeon this morning, and he answered all my last-minute questions. Dr. Buchmann is the reconstruction surgeon who will put me back together after Dr. Monroe takes things out (especially the cancer). I told the surgeons that if the operating room seemed a little crowded, it was because I had so many people sending prayers and angels to watch over us!

We then spent a leisurely few hours visiting the beautiful Loveland Living Planet Aquarium here in SLC. I especially loved watching the antics of the penguins and the shark tank tunnel! After that, we headed to IKEA. Believe it or not, I think I'm one of the few people my age who had never visited an IKEA store! It's probably a good thing that there's not one in Boise!

Well, I think I'll wrap this up. I have to check in at Huntsman at 6 a.m. tomorrow for a 7:45 surgery time. It's time to put this surgery in my "rearview mirror" and get on with the serious business of healing and working on finding my new voice. Happy Valentine's Day, and thank you all for the prayers, support, and love being sent my way. It means a lot to me.

—February 16, 2017

Good morning—this is Pam. John brought my laptop in, and you should see me trying to "hunt and peck" this entry! Between the oxygen sensor on my right middle finger, the splint on my left forearm, three drains, and several other tubes and lines, I keep coming up with some really weird text! It's a beautiful day here in SLC.

I am overwhelmed and humbled by all the prayers, good wishes, and love being sent my way. When John read me some of the posts on my first morning in ICU, I was filled with gratitude. How lucky I am to have so many good people in my life! The staff here is amazing—such talented and truly caring professionals. I know I have a long road ahead, but I feel I have already made great strides. Speaking of strides, I think it's time to take another stroll around the hallways—me and all my tubes! More later. Much love, Pam

—February 20, 2017

Happy President's Day! I think it's probably OK to use this title again. Looks like I may get to go back to Boise today! How fitting that would be—a holiday on my admission day and discharge day. Basically, we're waiting for a parade of various professionals to give us our "marching orders." There will be lots of care at home until we return for a follow-up appointment (probably March 2nd) and to get the rest of the sutures out, have a swallow study, and hopefully get the nose tube out.

I had some quiet time this morning to look fondly at these foothills out my window and review the amazing comments I have received on these posts. I am so grateful to John for helping keep everyone updated. You've probably learned more than you ever thought you would about laryngectomies! Maybe I should learn sign language for "TMI!"

Heartfelt thanks to all of you for your love and prayers and humor and virtual hugs that have helped keep my spirits up! Namaste.

—February 22, 2017

I wonder if anyone about to get married really understands the full meaning of the words, *for better or for worse*. All I can say is that I'm really glad that John not only said them but also meant them! It's been a pretty overwhelming re-entry into the real world. I see the engineering/mad scientist side of John as he mixes my food and medications and serves them to me at the appropriate time. I tease him about creating a spreadsheet to keep track of all these details! I marvel at his ability to function somewhat normally when I wake him from a sound sleep in the middle of the night.

I had no idea that the graft sites would cause me more discomfort than the stoma itself. I think I can empathize with anyone who has had a severe burn or a skin graft. But I am healing! Next week will be even better. I will have a swallow study and x-rays in SLC on March 1st and a doctor's appointment with suture removal on the 2nd. If all goes according to plan, he will take out the NG feeding tube, and I can slowly begin the work of learning to eat and speak.

For those of you who haven't been around me in person, I am using a Boogie Board for written communication. It's like a high-tech etch-a-sketch that you write on with a stylus and then push a button to clear it. In the hospital, they offered a small whiteboard with a vis-a-vis marker for patients to use. It was hard to take the cap off the marker. They were usually dried out, and they smelled! Needless to say, the staff was awed by this new gadget of mine. And guess who introduced me to it? Our granddaughters! Thank you, Rylie and Addie (and Geoff and Christine). On a side note, I've never gotten so many compliments on my penmanship!

That's it for now. I never tire of reading your comments. (They are like fuel to me!) Love and gratitude to you all!

Pam

—February 27, 2017

John asked me the question, "Do you miss being able to speak?" last night while we were watching the Oscars, and my answer surprised me (and him, I think!). "Not as much as I thought I would." Really? Really. I can think of things that I would miss more—not being able to see the smiling faces of people who are really glad to see me or the daffodil bulbs starting to break through the dusting of snow we got last night. Not being able to feel the hugs of my friends or the warmth of the sun coming in our window as I type this. Not being able to hear the voices of the people I care about or the music that fills our lives.

Of course, it's frustrating at times to not be able to blurt out a quick response (or retort). But being temporarily voiceless has taught me to think before I respond. What do I really want to say and how can I convey my message in the easiest, kindest way? Maybe I should have learned that lesson a long time ago. I'm sure I have caused some hurt feelings by talking before thinking. For that, I apologize. But for now, have patience with me as I write out my messages (in my beautiful penmanship) on my Boogie Board. I like to watch people predict what I'm going to write. Sometimes I'll even change what I was going to write just to keep them on their toes!

We're headed back to Salt Lake City tomorrow for appointments on Wednesday and Thursday. Hopefully I'll have some more positive updates for you then. In the meantime, thank you for being on this journey with me, and have a great day! Take the time to tell someone you love that you love them!

—March 1, 2017

A beautiful day in Salt Lake City, and we've been very busy. We spent several hours at Huntsman, and one of our tasks was to hand out thank you notes to many of the people who cared for me while I was in the hospital. John also had letters for some of the higher-ups in the hospital's administration. He has already heard back from some of them. It is amazing how much a simple "thank you" is appreciated!

So, my much-anticipated swallow study went well. I guess you could say I passed—meaning there were no leaks in my esophagus. So now the doctor wants me to eat/drink tonight, keep a food diary, let him know how it feels, and they will decide the next steps at tomorrow's appointment. One of the doctors wants to keep the feeding tube in until I can go a week or so eating and not losing weight. The other doctor is ready to let me get the tube out now. Most of the other practitioners are in the second camp and will be rooting for me tomorrow.

Tonight, John gets to go to a Utah Jazz basketball game, and I'm going to have a ladies' night in with my friend Jenny and her daughter Tessa. These are good friends who have opened their home to us during these trips to SLC. Like I've said before, we are blessed to have so many good people in our lives!

We plan to head home as soon as all the appointments are done tomorrow, and I plan to post again when we get back to Boise. I'm feeling good vibes for another good day tomorrow!

—March 7, 2017

Not sure where all the time goes, but I seem to be keeping pretty busy as I await the next milestones. So much to learn about the care and maintenance of my stoma and prosthesis. I'm trying to work on range of motion and strength exercises for my neck and wrist (from the graft). And then there's the food thing. It takes some planning to get all the daily calories and protein that the dieticians recommend. Of course, there's an app for that! And many thanks to our good friends (and son Geoff) who are keeping John well fed. Somehow, he's not too interested in joining me in my Boost Plus meals!

I've been venturing out a little more on my own. It's a little scary at first. A simple trip to the drug store isn't quite so simple. First, I write on my board, "Can I please get some help in cosmetics?" and show it to the man at the check stand. He calls someone over and informs her, "She has to write her question for you," in an overly loud voice. Anyway, I had the almost empty bottle of what I was looking for, but the clerk told me they didn't carry it anymore. After a few back-and-forth messages, she was able to find me a comparable product. We were both pleased. Mission accomplished!

I will try to keep this up to date as I figure out the next steps. I love reading your comments (and even just knowing that you care enough to be reading this). It helps me feel connected. Thank you! And so, it goes— moving forward with "baby steps"... Pam

The last big trip we took together was a month in New Zealand in February 2019. We'd never taken a vacation for this long, and the details worked out extremely well as we explored this beautiful country far away from Idaho. While we were there, we noticed some changes in the shape of Pam's stoma, but we were blissfully clueless as to the implications. It had changed shape slightly and seemed to bleed a lot easier. These were manageable symptoms, so we didn't give it much thought as we continued to experience and enjoy our adventure and savor the trip.

When we returned, a visit to our head and neck surgeon revealed that what we'd observed was not good; it was a return of Pam's cancer. This was devastating.

The only real option was the emerging field of immunotherapy, and Pam was approved for a monthly infusion of Keytruda that started in May of 2019. Statistics showed that this new type of therapy was effective in about 16 percent of cases, which told the engineer in me that they'd found a new therapy but didn't understand how it worked or on which patients. We were betting on a one-in-six chance, just like rolling dice. The odds didn't favor Pam, and within four months, we knew it hadn't worked. The rapid tissue growth around Pam's stoma continued, which resulted in her losing her airway right after our daughter's wedding. Her airway was extremely fragile, and they eventually inserted a tracheostomy tube. While this ensured that she could breathe with confidence, it silenced her voice forever.

There were a couple of milestone events during the summer of 2019, one being our daughter Jessica's wedding. Pam still had a voice at that time, but she had to use it sparingly, especially in a loud and crowded situation. She spent a lot of time with the bride, and while I was not privy to those conversations, our daughter subsequently told me how important and precious they were. Pam and I sat together at the ceremony and marveled at the beautiful young woman we'd raised and how much love and happiness she radiated that day. And we got to dance at the reception in Hinsdale. We'd always loved to get on the dance floor at weddings, and this one was supremely special. We quietly talked about our good fortune in finding each other long ago and about how proud we were of the people our children had become—intelligent and caring and committed to their families while striving to be outstanding American citizens. I will hold these private conversations close to my heart for the rest of my days.

Soon after the wedding, Pam lost all her verbal voicing capabilities. We hosted another reception in Boise for Jessica and Chris a couple of weeks later, and although Pam was still in OK shape, she was now effectively muted. So, conversations were held with me at her side or with her using her Boogie Board. I asked her if there was anything I could do for her that day, and she simply smiled and wrote that she wanted to take it all in and wasn't worried about her lack of a voice. We didn't get to hear Pam that day, but we were all keenly aware of her presence and glad she could join us.

I play in a jazz big band, and in August 2019, we had a performance at the Idaho Botanical Garden. Pam was beginning to slow down as the cancer advanced, but she was determined to be there and had invited several of her girlfriends to join her. So, I had a delightful gathering of women as a fan club that night. It was a beautiful summer evening in the Meditation Garden, and we played a three-set show until we ran out of light. There was lots of dancing in front of us, which is always a highlight for me to see and feel what kind of crowd response our music triggers, and we played a good show. But the lasting memory that I hold in my heart is looking out into the crowd in the middle of our second set and seeing Pam standing and smiling at me. She had lost her voice, but our eyes locked, and I almost missed my next entrance in playing the next song. No words, but an indelible memory of our deep connection.

It was clear that Pam was headed toward the finish line. Together, we decided to decline active therapy to give Pam the best quality of life. Hospice care at home was how this story would end. That care started in September. Now, all the nurses, aides, social workers, and meds would be delivered to Pam in our home. This also meant that I needed to develop a new set of caregiving tasks as Pam's physical decline accelerated throughout October. In the last three weeks, she could no longer communicate with the Boogie Board and was fully dependent on the nurses, aides, and me for her daily physical needs.

There were three or four times before October 31 when I felt I had almost lost her. In retrospect, I think she was trying on death and decided that she was not quite ready to go yet. Around 9:45 on Halloween night, I found her without a pulse, still warm. I'd been answering the door for trick-or-treaters and cleaning up in the kitchen. Pam had chosen to be alone when she transitioned to the other side, which I do believe was her way to protect me.

She had fought the good fight. I believe she had seen the destination. This loss was the beginning of my long journey toward transforming my life. Pam was my true love, and we were a team in battling through cancer, in finding sobriety together in 2011, and in creating a family and our lives together. I was now a widower and would never be the same guy again.

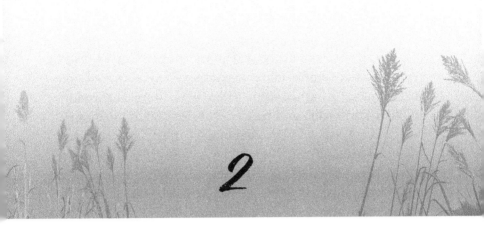

FAITH AND PERSPECTIVE RELATING TO MY THEOLOGY

The journey of processing grief prompted me to evaluate my faith. My theology hews pretty closely to United Methodist theology. I'm a preacher's kid, and I connected more closely with the details of the United Methodist faith tradition when I was posted in Penang, Malaysia, in 1996 as part of my job with HP. We'd planned to move production of a new hard disc drive to Penang to reduce production costs in this highly competitive market. Many of my colleagues in Malaysia were Muslims, and three of us American expats were invited to a Ramadan dinner one evening.

This turned out to be a seminal moment, as we had a respectful and comfortable conversation about faith traditions that evening. I learned a lot about Islam from Shahruddin, Bukhari, and Halim and realized that these kinds of conversations did not happen very often in the United States. Hmmm. Islam is a religion that is monotheistic, just like Christianity. They believe in one God that they call Allah. Their prophet was Mohammed, an illiterate shepherd who "authored" the Quran many years ago. They recognize Jesus Christ as another prophet. The big takeaway was that we believed many of the same things about faith and service to mankind, which are basic tenets of Islam and Christianity. In short, their beliefs were so similar to Christianity that it felt as if the only differences were the names of the relevant deities. These were faithful individuals who prayed five times a day, and we had graciously been invited to a meal with them during their holy month of Ramadan. After talking to these high-character individuals, I began to question the entire concept of Jesus being God's *only* son.

When we arrived at the restaurant, the tables were filled with platters of food, and a lot of discussion was underway at the restaurant. We found our dining partners quickly, and then a recorded voice came on the speakers and all conversation ceased. It was a local imam reciting the Shahada as the fourth prayer of the day. After this recitation was completed, the Muslims could break their fast and begin eating. Everyone was free to dive into the delicious platters of food. Halim excused himself after the recording ended, and I asked Shahruddin and Bukhari where he went. Halim wanted to grab a smoke before he started eating—something else they avoided until it was time to break their fast. He returned a few minutes later and joined us for that dinner.

When I came home that evening, I committed myself to understanding the core concepts of my United Methodist faith traditions in a deeper way. Over the next few months, some reading and discussions with Methodist theologians allowed me to find the details I was seeking. This included concepts of heaven, the nature of grace, and the basic historical nuts and bolts of Methodism. The experience also compelled me to teach confirmation at my home church in Boise for the next four years because my children were approaching the age of confirmation. Pam and I had met in MYF (Methodist Youth Fellowship) in 1972, and we wanted to teach our kids the faith traditions that we believed. It was time for me to step up and take action.

This was a satisfying endeavor that started with the confirmation of our son, Geoff, and ended four years later with the confirmation of our daughter, Jessica. We did not want to *tell* them what to believe; rather, we felt it was important to give them a comprehensive training in the faith tradition we'd chosen. This was meant to give them a theological source of comparison as they approached adulthood. It also meant getting them plugged into the church youth group, which was meaningful to both of us, since that's how we met.

How might I describe what United Methodist faith traditions looked like? I was asked to preach on this a few times on a lay Sunday when our pastor was away. I chose to start with the question, *Why do we do good deeds?* That's a loaded question, but I explained that, as it relates to United Methodist theology, there was, indeed, one right answer—an answer I thought was not well understood by a lot of Americans. That answer was also the basis of how I taught several confirmation class lessons and was a way of defining my faith.

The simple answer is that we do good deeds as a means of saying *thank you* to the Almighty for the universal love and forgiveness we are all offered. The apostle Paul wrote about this in Romans when he asserted that we are justified by faith and not by deeds. I believe that God knows me by name and that

I am already loved and forgiven for all the actions in my life—before I even ask for that love and forgiveness. This is called *prevenient grace,* and it leads to the conclusion that everyone is going to heaven after death. That's one of the more challenging aspects of the United Methodist faith tradition because it means we cannot *earn* our way into heaven.

We discussed this almost every week in confirmation class. I asked the confirmands how to earn "heaven points." And with a wink and a smile, I reminded them that this was not the way it worked.

This precept turns behavior choices upside down for a lot of people—for a lot of committed Christians—which was why I presented this theme from the pulpit numerous times. We needed to be reminded of this less-than-intuitive set of beliefs. When I/we know that God is already in our corner and that our place in heaven is assured, the whole picture changes. We look at service to our hometowns and to the underprivileged around the world as a vehicle for saying *thank you* to God for this incredible gift of grace. When we screw up, we can acknowledge our mistakes and repent of them, then get back to living a faithful life. We are already forgiven for these transgressions, and we know that we cannot earn our way into heaven.

These beliefs put me on a very solid foundation for living my life. I'm not concerned with being good enough to go to heaven. I know how huge this gift of universal love and forgiveness is. Gratitude takes the form of serving in a soup kitchen, sharing financially through offerings at church or donations to UMCOR's (United Methodist Committee on Relief) projects around the globe, walking in the CROP Hunger Walk, or raking leaves for seniors during Rake Up Boise. There's no guilt associated with this theology; it focuses on gratitude and on the rock-solid belief that God knows me and wants to position me for a full life of joyful service. That theology defined how I lived my life and how we raised our children. I have deep confidence that God is in my corner at all times and wants me to succeed and serve others.

My faith was important as Pam and I went through the hospice experience. And it took some interesting turns in the months after she died. But I was confident that she was headed to a better place and that all the pain and infirmity she'd endured would disappear after she departed in spirit. This was foundational in allowing me to navigate the chaos in my head and in my heart after she died. I was grateful to be clear about these beliefs.

When Pam died, I believe several mental circuit breakers blew open in my brain—a survival mechanism for experiencing this level of grief without absolutely blowing apart. But once a bit of rational thought began returning to me, I felt a deep anger toward God and His perceived role in *taking* Pam from me. That anger was white hot, and the best way I can describe it is that I was unable to have a civil conversation (prayer, monologue, etc.) with God for a very long time. I needed to address this issue, and my grief therapist offered me some initial perspective to begin the process of dealing with heavy and overwhelming emotions. I believe this is where the right side of my brain began to slowly wake up.

My training and history as a left-brain, problem-solving engineer was not well suited for what I needed to learn and accept. It became clear that if I was going to continue to move forward, I would always lead with my head for the rest of my days, but I also needed to engage my heart and the right hemisphere of my brain.

I told my grief therapist that my anger stopped me in my tracks and prevented me from making progress on my journey, and she asked some interesting questions.

"Can you see God walking next to you to help ease the pain?"

My answer at that time was an emphatic, "No!"

"Can you see anyone walking next to you to ease the pain?" she asked.

I had some friends who were keeping an eye on me, so I said, "Yes."

Then she suggested that God might be working through these individuals to ease my pain. That resonated with me and got me moving toward some intimation of healing.

One of my next epiphanies came from feedback from my brother Pete. I'd been attending a series of gatherings known as Grief Share, and these were marginally helpful but often not something that I could relate to well. One of the sessions addressed the book of Job as a metaphor and example of rising from significant tragedy and grief. I dug into that Old Testament book, and I was not at all motivated by this story. In the latter part of the book, God appears to be rubbing Job's nose in his lack of faith after being betrayed by friends and losing everything. The God of retribution was not the Almighty I knew.

My brother pointed me toward the Gospel of John, chapter 9. In this story, we find Jesus and the disciples coming upon a blind man. One of the disciples asked Christ if it was this man's sin or his father's sin that caused him to be blind from birth. Now we had a story that wasn't written by another human (as in the case of Job) but one which had a direct quote from the Son of God, so I paid much closer attention.

Jesus's response was, "This man was blind for the greater glory of God."

The problem was that we humans couldn't see the big picture or the overriding plan. Christ then spit in the dust, made a mud pie, smeared it on the man's eyes, and restored his sight. This quote and its source are what brought about an epiphany.

I then came to believe that Pam was taken from Earth in part because she was needed somewhere else. This is part of that big plan that I simply cannot see. I do *not* believe that the Almighty caused Pam's cancer. That event was not part of that mysterious plan that isn't within my sight or understanding. I believe she is pain free and is in a place defined by love. These components of my theology survived the devastating pain of her death.

But even though those thoughts were in my head, it took a long time for me to put Pam in that picture and for the whole concept to reach my heart. Moving from my head to my heart was a process of taking theological, theoretical thoughts and turning them into a true heartfelt belief with Pam at the center of the picture. I was still a left-brain engineer, and this demanded that I confront my faith to truly believe that my departed spouse was in a spiritual afterlife. That test was more daunting than I would have ever imagined, despite being a life-long Christian.

I had to get to a point where I trusted the Almighty. I had to get to a point (much more difficult and a process that continues to this day) where I saw Pam as someone/something that was not *taken from me*. This meant that I had to admit that she was never really mine in the first place—a very tough pill to swallow. When I was able to make that transition and understand that it was *my* faith that needed to make the shift from a left-brain mental concept to a heartfelt belief deep in my soul, then I could start making progress.

My faith journey continues, and I now see that this path will never end. My faith continues to evolve, and it continues to influence my behaviors and my life choices. It really is all about the journey and not about the destination. I'm glad I have this faith to lean into as I navigate the journey of grief.

GRIEF ILLITERACY

In Megan Devine's book *It's OK That You're Not OK: Meeting Grief and Loss in a Culture That Doesn't Understand*, she addresses the concept of *grief illiteracy*. I define this as the inability to understand the impact of loss and act accordingly. Her concept is linked to American culture and was a message that stuck with me in the months following Pam's death. My self-image had always been based on being dependable, on being someone you could count on. This was how I was measured at work, but it was also the kind of person I wanted to be. Certainly, my view of myself (by definition) was not an objective one, but I had this as a general goal, and I believed I was doing a relatively good job of delivering on it.

The corollary to this was that I strove to be someone who was rarely in a position where I needed someone else's assistance. I wanted to be the guy who offered help. When I was active in my career and service work, my left-brain universe was fulfilled by competence, being viewed as dependable, and achieving my goals. I was secure in my volunteer work and family life; I was a happy man.

When I became a widower, the entire structure of my world crumbled. For the first time in my adult life, I had significant needs, and I was in no position to figure out how to meet them. I wanted to understand what had happened. I was forced to envision a future for myself without Pam. I wanted to learn to accept this disaster that I couldn't change. There were dozens of other issues that I couldn't articulate to myself or anyone else. These issues included how I viewed myself in this new reality, how I was going to effectively support my children as they faced the loss of their mother, and what was going to happen next in my life now that Pam was no longer by my side. I had simply never given much thought to these decisions because I had been so focused on being the best caregiver I could be while Pam was still alive. I had no idea how I was going to meet these types of goals. My view of goals was that, when I chose to pursue certain outcomes, I wanted to do the best job of achieving them that I could. I wanted to demonstrate competence and resilience, and I wanted to choose carefully what was to be next for me. Who was I going to be now that I was a widower? How would I live a life that approximated being a role model for others? How would I address the deep pain in my heart? This was all new territory for me because Pam was no longer in my day-to-day life. My heart was broken in a way I'd never experienced. And although I didn't fully understand it at that time, my brain was working at a significantly degraded level. This was related to those mental circuit breakers I've mentioned blowing open, but I didn't understand this until many months after Pam died. My emotions were raw, and my cognitive functioning was diminished.

The COVID-19 pandemic invaded our lives in March 2020, and the related isolation made everything worse. I was alone, and my phone was awfully quiet. Didn't my friends understand that *this* was the time that I needed them? Simply checking in with me would have been sufficient to meet my needs. My self-esteem was at rock bottom, and I was seriously unprepared for what I needed to do to start healing from this train wreck.

My silent phone and my own (perhaps unrealistic) expectations led me to a place of feeling angry and invisible. There were a few friends who called, but from my point of view, the list was really short. That anger fed right into what I was feeling toward the Almighty in terms of Pam being taken from me via this heartless and cruel disease. When I read the thesis from Ms. Devine relating to grief illiteracy, I fully agreed. Many of my friends had no idea about the depth of pain I was feeling, and they apparently weren't interested in reaching out and helping me through this disastrously unique time.

I discussed this with my grief counselor, and some empowering actions started to take shape. My first realization was that all these people were also experiencing deep grief due to Pam's death. She'd been an extraordinary person and friend, and they also had to process her departure. When I became a bit more rational, I understood that these friends were also very busy people who had lives of their own that continued. My life had come to a halt. Theirs had not, and there were things they had to attend to.

But the piece that truly propelled me into a better space was to convince myself, per author Brené Brown's writings, that everyone was doing the best that he or she could under the circumstances. I wasn't always successful in achieving this, but when I was, these thoughts about my seemingly absent friends allowed me to avoid the anger and put the whole scenario in a much more charitable frame.

I remember being on my back deck and coming to the next step in this progression. I still harbored a component of anger that I hadn't been able to stop cancer from taking Pam.

When I screamed at God, it often took the form of, "I did not get a vote here!" So, I was always thinking about how I could move forward in a manner that felt empowered. How could I get a vote and decide what would be next?

If everyone was doing the best that they could, but I still had unmet needs in this journey, what could I do about it? That answer became clear to me in early 2021. What if I approached these individuals and asked for help in a more specific way? This idea appealed to me. I could choose who was on that list, and I would make the first move and acknowledge what I needed. And I could craft a pitch that I hoped they would agree to.

The list contained about forty names. My need and my request would be simple. *Could you call me or email me monthly, more or less, to simply check in?* I prefaced this with the story of how I came to the point of asking this and that he or she was on my list of most admired people. All the responses here were an enthusiastic YES! I felt very good about this because I'd found a way to express my needs that would help toward healing, and I took action.

Most of those friends still keep in touch with me on a regular basis. Interestingly, making that request took a large chunk of the venom out of my previous frustrations. If they didn't call or email, I found that I was OK with that. I now had direct feedback from them, and I knew which of these friends intended to maintain contact with me, the new widower. I found that this was enough, no matter what their actual follow-up was. Now I could move forward and relegate the grief illiteracy concept to my rearview mirror. This progression also put me in a position to see and feel the loving support I'd received from so many more clearly. I was a fortunate man to have friends and family members who truly cared about me. Before, I hadn't been in a state of mind and heart to see this clearly.

The changes that occurred along this part of my journey often were initiated in anger, but I don't want that to be the main message here. I learned to understand and manage my anger much better as I continued to read about grief. I committed to paying better attention to what I felt, and I discovered that I was more empowered to address strong emotions than I'd previously thought. I just needed to let trusted people know that I was vulnerable. When I told my friends how they could help me in an explicit manner, they were more than happy to step up and offer that support. They simply hadn't known what I needed.

Those periodic contacts have now evolved into more transparent and authentic friendships. We have discussions about emotions and grief, which are part of all our lives. These relationships were deepened by the shared experience of Pam's death. It's still very hard for me to see blessings that came forth from the worst thing that ever happened to me, but this is one of them. This was a major discovery for me, and although it took the better part of two years to put those pieces together in a way that I could understand adequately, I now appreciate what I've gained.

I can now speak openly about Pam, and I even initiate conversations about her, which helps others feel more comfortable talking about her. I realize that people don't want to resort to offering clichés, so they often don't say anything. But talking about my feelings of grief opens conversations and represents effective healing.

I understand grief illiteracy better now, and I take action to counter it when it makes sense for my well-being.

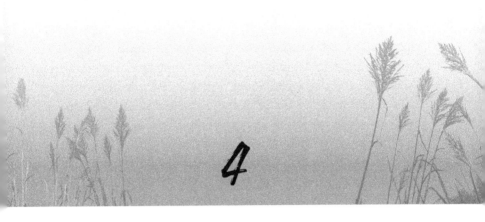

LEFT BRAIN AND RIGHT BRAIN LEARNINGS

As I understand it, there's both physiology as well as a good measure of popular myth regarding left brain vs. right brain. I don't want to make a judgment on these myths but would like to explain some of what I've learned.

The physiology of the human brain shows that the left hemisphere controls the right side of the body. Data also indicates that understanding numbers, math, language skills, and analytical thinking have their origins in the left hemisphere. The right hemisphere has control over the left side of the body and is the home to concepts such as expression, emotional intelligence, imagination, and creativity.

The media and some pundits have taken this a step further and declared that being left-brained is associated with logical thinkers and organized individuals, while those categorized as right-brained are artists and creatives. A study on the WebMD website sought to debunk this all-or-nothing categorization. In short, it stated that what we know about how the brain works is *a lot* more complex than this simple nomenclature. The study asserts that the brain is incredibly flexible (a term called plasticity) and can adapt to injuries or significant psychological stresses by forming new neural pathways when and where needed.

Let's stay with this overly simplified definition. I was raised to be a dependable, high-achieving individual. I was competitive and oriented toward a successful career when I chose mechanical engineering as my major in college. I received a strong message from my parents that going to college would take me to a chosen career path, and I heard this loud and clear. I was good at math, I understood science, and I enjoyed being a problem solver. My dad and my older brother were chemical engineers. Through them, I experienced the kind of career and lifestyle that was available to an engineer, and this appealed to me. So, I went off to university in 1976 and spent two years at the University of Minnesota and the final two at the University of Illinois. Pam and I moved in together in Champaign those last two years and were married on May 31, 1980, thirteen days after I graduated.

In 1980, it was a terrific year to get an engineering degree, and I had five or six job offers to choose from. Furthermore, I'd completed a summer intern position with Ford Motor Company in Dearborn, Michigan, in 1979. This experience differentiated me in interviews, and I could speak to projects like cost reduction, yield optimization, and meeting critical production deadlines from my summer work in the light truck division at Ford. I caught a couple of crucial good breaks, and in the spring of 1980, I accepted a job offer from Hewlett Packard's Disc Memory Division (DMD) in Boise, Idaho.

HP's management approach had garnered high praise and a lot of emulation by other firms. It was often called "The

HP Way," and it was summed up as MBO, Management by Objectives. I met with my immediate supervisor on a regular basis, and we discussed what deliverables I needed to prioritize. He offered ideas on how to meet those objectives, but the primary onus was on me to figure out how to achieve the measurable goals. This was an ideal environment for my work style. It started with the inherent trust HP had in my abilities. They hired me to utilize the left side of my brain and for my enthusiastic motivation to achieve. Now I was to put these skills to work in service to the business goals at HP.

I thrived in this environment. I was reminded to ask for help when I needed it and to maintain high business ethics and was then turned loose to show my management team what I could do. I loved this problem-solving space that was built on management's trust and belief in my skills. I usually showed up at work, raring to go, determined to show them what I could deliver. There were many successes in those first few years in terms of cost reductions and yield improvements. I enjoyed excellent working relationships between production workers, management, and production engineers such as myself. These types of working relationships had been lacking at Ford, and I was pleased to be a part of a team that was pointed in the same direction and worked together in a seamless manner. This success also showed up in my paycheck, which was one more reason to keep doing what I was doing.

I share this history because it hardwired my brain's functioning. I was no longer a student competing for grades. I was now part of a large and well-respected multinational corporation. My actions and achievements were directly reflected in the bottom-line performance of my division within HP. And I was surrounded by other young professionals like myself who were early in their careers, far from home, and starting new lives in a new city. All of this turned me into a card-carrying left-hemisphere kind of guy.

I believe my right brain slowly started to wake up when I lived a sober lifestyle from 1999 until 2006. This process continued when I got sober again in 2011. I had to acknowledge the less-than-ideal patterns in my life and in my flawed thinking that led to the abuse of alcohol. When I quit drinking, I fundamentally differentiated myself from a lot of my old friends. As I often heard at Alcoholics Anonymous (AA) meetings, I had to change my playmates, my playgrounds, and my play dates to position myself for success in saying goodbye to alcohol. That meant understanding myself in a more self-reflective manner and invoking right-brain skills, such as emotional intelligence.

My right brain got another boost when I went through my cancer therapy. I wasn't sure I was going to survive that health adventure, so I had to get my affairs in order. And this had to occur while I was fundamentally beaten up from the radiation and chemotherapies meant to help me to become cancer free. I recognized and acknowledged that I wasn't the same person that I'd been before treatment. Becoming a cancer survivor and having the opportunity to confront my mortality triggered some primary changes within me. I came to fully understand how to be in the moment and embrace gratitude whenever I could. Those right-brain insights were incredibly important in 2015 when Pam and I swapped chairs of patient and caregiver. And again in 2017, when Pam needed my help to recover from her laryngectomy.

In 2019, some of the most significant changes occurred in my thinking and in my demeanor. Hospice changed me, but the big blow was yet to come. How could I move forward after Pam died? My grief counseling was key during many moments when I was confronted with confusion and pain. Reading about grief gave me some tools to better understand this experience and to position myself to make good decisions about what was next for me.

I began to recognize that empathy—a right-brain quality—was awakening in me. My interpretation was that a significant and deeply painful event had occurred that caused me to embrace right-brain behaviors and patterns. My heart had been broken, and then it had been opened. I became much more self-aware regarding emotions.

I wrote about this on Caring Bridge after seeing a piece on CNN about empathy. I believed that a large majority of men had done what I'd done—leaned into a left-brain lifestyle. We couldn't change or even recognize this pattern until we'd been dropped to our knees by a cataclysmic event like losing a spouse. I still believe this to be accurate. I'm a very different man because of what I went through in losing Pam. I would not be this guy unless something had blown my life and my ego-based left brain to pieces.

So, even if my simplified description of right brain vs. left brain is not totally accurate from a medical view, the metaphor is useful. I now have my *heart* involved in decisions and in my perception of the world around me. I know that I lead with my head, but my right brain is now an active part of how I experience the world and what I decide. It's been an awakening, which is an extraordinary thing to ponder. I'm different now, and the changes continue to occur. But I think I can see where I want to go, and I will leverage that intent when I can.

I also observe things differently now and ponder them from a new point of view. I want to lean in when I see people in pain. In the past, someone else's pain wouldn't have registered with me. I want to leave things better than I found them, and this often takes the form of improving someone's day or simply listening well to the stories they share. My default compulsion to fix an issue has evaporated. I see sitting and feeling with another as a gift from my right brain.

I recently read a remarkable book called *My Stroke of Insight: A Brain Scientist's Personal Journey* by Jill Bolte Taylor, Ph.D.

It's a riveting account of a brain researcher who experienced a stroke in her left hemisphere. Her professional knowledge allowed her to bring a unique perspective on the story of the event and the long rehab process afterward. It's a story of transformation, and it resonated with me in many ways.

Her descriptions of the functions of the left and right sides of her brain are detailed and compelling. She recounts the overall organizational functions that originate on the left side. In her case, speaking and understanding language and numbers were an effective way of sharing her knowledge of how the left brain worked. The left brain also housed her professional knowledge and her memories of experiences, colleagues, and general information related to how we live our lives. This is where the primary damage from her unique flavor of stroke occurred.

The brain tissue damage manifested in her being thrust into a full-on right-brain set of experiences, and she came to understand these as a form of nirvana. There was peace, silence, and a lack of pain and worry when she was in her right brain. Eventually, this glimpse of what was available to her at any time was one of the most profound understandings of her life-changing experience. All it took for her to return to that extremely pleasant place of peace and of being one with the Universe was to conjure up an intent to dive deeper into the right side of her brain. That revelation stopped me in my tracks, and I had to put her book down for a few minutes. Was this akin to what I was experiencing as I leaned into the changes I was going through?

That chapter on "What I Needed Most" was meant to educate all readers about how one could interact effectively and compassionately with stroke victims. She wanted us to understand these details because stroke is so common. But I found myself reading these suggestions with different eyes than I might have had before losing Pam. In the same chapter, she also said that she was never going to be the same person again after this experience. This included what she chose as her path forward.

That's exactly what I'm experiencing now and what I wish to share with you. In my right brain awakening, I wish to be a much kinder and more empathic individual. I know there's a lot of room for growth in these spaces, but it's who I want the new John to represent.

Kindness and empathy were central to Dr. Taylor when deciding whom she could trust. She explained the kind of energy that different people brought into her life. This powerfully resonated with me in many ways. In later chapters, I explain how I chose to include certain people in my life as a way of pushing back against loneliness and isolation. I wanted to populate my life with high-character people who I trusted and admired. It's not a stretch to align this desire with Dr. Taylor's intent to have people in her life who bring positive energy.

I want to be that kind of person on a consistent basis. I wanted to deliver positive energy every time I could. I saw this in my desire to leave positive ripples in my wake with casual encounters. It was also the underpinnings of my intent to become a better listener and to be the kind of friend everyone would consciously want in their lives.

I knew the old John was gone after Pam died. And I discovered that, as my brain awakened after the disaster of her death, I had the power to choose what my path forward would look like. Change would inevitably occur in me. Early on, I concluded that this was a critical time for me to make some good decisions about the nature of that change. I wanted to let this new right brain awakening unfold, and I wanted to let it take me in a new direction. I wanted to become a new person who regularly delivered the benefit of the doubt, love, and understanding to others. Dr. Taylor's book gave me a new perspective on those choices. It also educated me on the physiology of my brain and what roles it played in my transformation.

GRIEF, GOALS, AND GRATITUDE

How I view myself from day to day can change dramatically. I'm the youngest of four children of Norm and Shirley Lodal. My oldest sister, Claire, died of cancer. Beth and Pete are still here. Both our parents are now gone. There are days when I feel like I'm the old soul of this remaining trio. I have seen, felt, and experienced things that neither of my surviving siblings has. I often feel that *no one* knows me now. Many times, this can veer into thoughts of me not knowing *myself* in any kind of accurate fashion. The ongoing struggles I have in accepting Pam's death contribute to this because I'd been in love with her since I was fourteen.

There are other days when I feel like the stereotypical youngest child. I feel like I don't know much of anything and that I'm supposed to know more at sixty-four years old. I then recognize that I'm not being very kind to myself. So, the next step becomes to draw different conclusions and cut myself some slack.

A widow once told me that she felt like she'd lost her big toe when her husband died. That metaphor seems accurate to me. I often feel unbalanced and less than fully authentic—feelings you might have to manage if you were, indeed, missing a big toe.

On the positive side, I'm proud of what I've decided to prioritize. My service through my Rotary club and being on the board of the NGO Semilla Nueva (a non-profit organization that works to develop bio-fortified corn in Guatemala to address the generations-long issue of widespread malnutrition in that country) allows me to tangibly leave the world better than I found it. It is that motto, *He strove to leave it better than he found it,* that will appear on Pam's and my shared companion post at the cemetery when I depart this life.

I continue to pursue other goals, and one of those is music. I'm a trombone player in the jazz big band called Boise Straight Ahead. We're a group of about twenty musicians, and we've been playing together since 1997. The band started out as all HP employees. At first, we decided we wouldn't accept performance fees since we were all gainfully employed. But eventually, since we didn't want to be known as "that free band," we asked our hosts to make a minimum donation of $1,000 to the United Way in our name. Over the years, we've raised over $100,000 for various non-profits (Boys and Girls Clubs, Idaho Botanical Gardens, etc.) around the Treasure Valley in southwest Idaho. I've always valued the focus I conjure up when we're on stage. Now, I value this same single-minded focus when we rehearse. I love that I can always count on big smiles when I see a dance floor full of happy people.

This is but one component of the pieces of my new life. In my more cynical (yet oddly accurate at times) moods, I see these activities as *distractions* that take my mind away from the pain and grief of no longer having Pam by my side. I don't mean to minimize the good work that I'm part of, but these activities are distractions that give my mind and heart a bit of a rest from the hard journey of grief. I believe that without them, I'd fall into a state of clinical depression.

There's a mental health management angle that took me a while to fully comprehend. It started with me actively choosing what would be next and then leaning into those choices. That was the easy part. Knowing what might have happened to my mental health had I *not* taken these steps was more challenging. So, I offer this question to the reader: *What might you wish to do now that your old life is gone?* Your answers can bring some enjoyment back to you as the griever. They could also allow you to sidestep future issues that would negatively affect your quality of life. The answers are empowering, they are important, and they are yours to own.

My new role as the incoming president of my Rotary club will demand that I embrace leadership qualities. Part of me will find this easy to do, but there are some related challenges. This is where the perspective I've learned as a widower will hopefully come in handy. In short, I am striving to be a better listener. I think I have capable collaboration skills. But opening to the thoughts and aspirations of others (of those I want to lead effectively) is going to take some conscious intent and effort.

The topic of control is something I've spent a fair amount of time pondering on my back deck. I like to think of myself as a good planner, and I get great satisfaction when I see a plan come together. I often wonder how much control I actually have in this life. I like to feel in control when I can, so I continue to strive for this objective. I like to do the things that I've chosen to do. These can include service, entertainment, travel, or time with friends and family. When I look back on my life, it appears that good planning (and a lot of good luck) have allowed me a level of control that is pleasing. But I didn't get a vote regarding Pam's death, and I'm still a long way from accepting that sad event. That's why I continue to wonder if I have any control over life at all.

As I entered the third year of widowerhood, I asked my grief counselor what I might establish as goals now that Pam had been gone for this long. Her answer, as usual, was right on the money. She told me to ask myself, "What role is Pam going to play in my life going forward?" That question immediately resonated with me. I knew I was going to have to sit with this for a while. I decided this was a very empowering question. I got to *choose* the answers, and I had a vast library of pleasant memories from which to choose. Although I didn't get a vote regarding her death, I now had the *only* vote about how I chose to remember her and what role she would play in the new version of me that was emerging.

This was another significant epiphany for me. It was a combination of the left-brain engineer that I was and the right-brain guy I was becoming. It was up to me to sort out the answer. I had a challenging and relevant goal to pursue, and I needed to give my head and my heart enough time and space to compile the answers. This fed me and was a positive influence on my self-image. And my self-image shifted around a lot more than I would have imagined.

I don't have a final answer to this question, but I'm finding ways to enjoy the process of answering it. I can ponder who and what Pam was, as well as the nature of the life we built together. I can see an answer when I speak to my children and see how they're raising our grandchildren. There are many shared travel adventures that I can revisit whenever I wish. I can embrace deep gratitude for having been allowed to live and share life with such an extraordinary person for thirty-nine years.

I've found great satisfaction in honoring Pam since I lost her. Her name is now on two bridges in Boise. We share a new paver at the Anne Frank Memorial in Boise and are sponsoring a new piece of art celebrating Hope at the Wassmuth Center for Human Rights in Boise. There will be a handsome new park along the Boise River that will carry Pam's name and will also honor peace and environmental sustainability and wetland preservation. When I worship, I now light a candle and spend time thinking of her and us. And I strive to say her name aloud often because this fills my heart and keeps her present to me in a meaningful way.

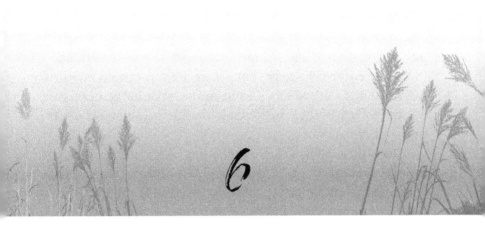

GRIEF LITERATURE
AND A NEW
PERSPECTIVE

M Y head and my heart began coming back online a few months after Pam's death, and I was finally able to do some reading. There seems to be a deep, organic process as to when the timing of a particular grief-related book will speak to one's heart and soul. The first book I read was *It's OK That You're Not OK: Meeting Grief and Loss in a Culture That Doesn't Understand* by Megan Devine. Then I read two books by Tom Zuba: *Permission to Mourn: A New Way to Do Grief* and *Becoming Radiant: A New Way to Do Life Following the Death of a Beloved*. These were followed by *Rising Strong: How the Ability to Reset Transforms the Way We Live, Love, Parent, and Lead* by Brené Brown. And then *The Grace in Dying* by Kathleen Dowling Singh. Each book taught me some valuable lessons about my new status and allowed me to consider new ways of thinking and new behaviors. In short, these authors offered me the opportunity to develop a different perspective now that I was a widower. Each author was credible because they'd experienced the same type of loss as me.

The first powerful, new thought came from Megan Devine, and this was her explanation of Pain vs. Suffering. Her husband had died in an accident that she had witnessed. After that, Devine asserted that pain couldn't be avoided; pain will find a way to manifest and can lead to other issues later in the griever's life if not dealt with at the onset. Her suggested path forward was to invite the pain to sit with you.

She said, "Look at it directly and tell it that you know it's not going anywhere. Commit to the intent that you will acknowledge it and wrestle with it and NOT ignore it."

I took Devine at her word and always kept an extra chair on my back deck, so Pain could join me at any time. I was experiencing a deep emotional and physical sorrow that wouldn't subside, and I needed strategies to address the fifty-ton weight that constantly bore down on my chest. My left-brain, problem-solving nature couldn't be effective this time; I saw no way to fix what was broken. I simply had to engage the pain and listen to my heart.

I needed to pay attention and let the grieving process proceed at whatever pace it chose. It took me eight months to realize that part of me had died with Pam on October 31, 2019. This was a conundrum to my engineering brain. Why did this seemingly obvious conclusion take so long for me to realize? I think it's related to my mental circuit breakers slowly clicking back into a closed and working position, many of which blew wide open when Pam died. For example, it took at least thirty minutes for me to call anyone (hospice, my son, my daughter) after I discovered that Pam had passed away. My brain had fuzzed out in the face of an overwhelming reality. I didn't know how much of my normal cognitive functioning appeared to have gone offline until months later. These open circuit breakers were a tangible defense mechanism for my mental health. The pace at which they closed again was something I had little or no control over. I simply had to pay attention to what I was feeling and experiencing, then let the process play out at its own pace. Engaging pain with my eyes and heart wide open was instrumental in moving forward. This wasn't easy. It required conscious intent and fortitude.

Ms. Devine's concept of suffering was one I could understand and embrace without much effort, and this was one part of my journey through grief where my left-brain tendencies served me well. Suffering involves aspects of one's life that *can* be actively addressed. Thus, many parts of suffering could be avoided or actively opposed. For me, suffering included things like sleeping poorly and erratic eating habits. I found myself resonating with this concept because it was empowering. It was something I could actively address with skills I'd honed before Pam's death.

I almost always ate a decent breakfast, but it was a crapshoot from day to day regarding what and how much I ate the rest of that day. I lost about twenty pounds. Gradually, I learned how to grocery shop for only myself. I embraced physical fitness and physical activity in a robust manner, and I often found myself on my bike or on my skis. I lifted weights and used exercise bands at home on a regular basis. I had some personal choices to make, and admittedly, there was an intriguing level of freedom that was now central in my life.

I was able to sleep, but those sleep patterns had changed dramatically during our hospice experience. Sleep was a multi-layered issue for me. As Pam's physical decline accelerated, one of the greatest immediate health threats was the clogging of her trach tube. This was usually related to dried mucus, and I was on point to fix it when it happened. There were a few ways I

could reduce its frequency or urgency, but I could never elimi-
nate the threat. Pam couldn't do this on her own in the last
three to four weeks of her life, so I developed some necessary
and highly sensitive listening skills. I could hear when a blockage was developing by listening closely to Pam's breathing. The
most urgent issues often came in the middle of the night, and
I was frequently awakened to an urgent trach tube blockage
that took me from a dead sleep to being fully awake and taking
action within seconds. The third time this happened, I decided
I wouldn't allow myself to sleep deeply. And I didn't. But for a
long time after she was gone, I couldn't fall into a deep sleep. I
imagine this was a PTSD response to all that I'd experienced.
I'd done what had to be done while she was still alive, but I
couldn't easily turn it off when I was no longer a caregiver.
Thus, one flavor of suffering continued as I stumbled forward
on my journey of grief.

I had hoped to see Pam in my dreams and that I would
remember those dreams. This has not turned out to be the
case. I dream infrequently, and Pam is rarely in the dreams
that I can remember. I'm a morning person, so I rise early, and
the house is very quiet at that time of day. Most mornings,
within a few minutes of waking up, I'm reminded that I'm
alone—and would rather not be. In that brief but surprisingly
consistent wave of acute pain, I consider my time asleep as a
respite when I'm not burdened by thoughts of grief and related
pain. When I'm asleep, I'm temporarily freed from grief. I quietly acknowledge this fact, express gratitude for my sleep, and
then move forward into whatever awaits that day.

After losing Pam, one of my Rotary colleagues gave me a
pair of remarkable books by Tom Zuba: *Permission to Mourn* and
Becoming Radiant. Zuba had been featured by Oprah Winfrey,
so his books had experienced commercial and critical success.

Zuba's biography is heartbreaking and absolutely grabbed
my attention in an overwhelming manner. He lost an

eighteen-month-old daughter. A few years later, his wife died suddenly. A few years after that, his thirteen-year-old son died. Even in my diminished mental and emotional state, I recognized that this man had experienced a trifecta of pain, heartache, and personal disaster that could not be ignored.

My Rotary colleague had been a high-level and very highly respected manager of the National Interagency Fire Center (NIFC) in Boise, Idaho. He had some fascinating career stories, but most importantly, he's a compassionate person who recognized how destroyed I was. I vaguely recall him pressing a reusable grocery bag containing the books into my hands at the first Rotary meeting I attended after Halloween. That bag made it to my family room and didn't budge for another few months. Steve told me that the NIFC gave these two books to families of firefighters who'd died in the line of duty.

Zuba's style is akin to poetry. The books can be consumed quickly because the text isn't dense, but I didn't approach them in this manner. His biography and searing personal grief were close at hand as I read his words. Amid all the pain and grief, he'd found a new way to grieve as he mourned departed members of his nuclear family. This helped me a lot in terms of framing my process in 2020.

His unique writing style was well suited for my detonated brain and heart. However, when I revisited these books two years later, I saw them with new eyes and found even deeper insights. It was a means of seeing how much I'd changed since the first reading.

I'd had some experience in this space of self-reflection relating to a TED Talk on grief by Nora McInerny. I saw Nora's YouTube video right after Pam died, and it was helpful. Then I stumbled across it again on the NPR TED radio hour in 2020. When I heard her TED Talk the second time, it was accompanied by a commentary from her, and I recognized how much I'd already changed since I heard it the first time on my laptop. I now had a personal perspective on grief and had logged my own miles in defining how I would change my life going forward.

Reading Tom Zuba's book a second time was an even more dramatic experience. It felt like I was much more ready to internalize and fully accept many of these concepts when I reread them. The first time, I was primarily relieved to know that these creative individuals had experienced what I was going through in such a graceful and helpful manner. I was *not* alone. I absorbed their experiences emotionally, not cognitively.

Consistent with the title of the book, I was reminded of how important it was to get into the pit with my dark and sad feelings about losing my true love. I gave myself permission to re-enter this space and experience it again. I'd already done a lot of this, but it was clear that I could revisit this wrestling even more. It was a way to look at my emotions and feel them with my new eyes and recognize how much I had already changed. In short, I still had a lot of work to do, but I also knew that I was far removed from that devastated and nearly paralyzed widower of late 2019.

Zuba claimed that it was good to try to nudge myself toward the belief that *Pam's life had been the perfect length.* There was a lot of theology in his work, and it started with my faith that the Almighty was indeed an all-loving entity. I'm still digesting the idea that her life was the perfect length, and it's taking me down a good path—one that I'm now willing to be led into.

Zuba also claimed that my relationship with Pam did *not* come to an end when she died. Part of me has always believed this, and he pressed this point hard. My heart seems ready to *try* to believe that she's here with me now in a way that I cannot fully understand, and I realize that the nature of our altered relationship is up to my decisions going forward. This relates to answering the question my grief counselor asked about what role Pam will now play in my life. In a simplified description, I now have choices about addressing my grief with memories of the adventures we shared and by leaning into the concept that she is still here with me in some fashion that I'm still coming to understand and appreciate.

Many aspects of this journey cause me to question the nature of my faith. Whether that's theological faith or my belief about what happens after we depart this life, it boils down to sorting out what I believe. And then I get to analyze how strong that faith is.

Zuba references this in a couple of ways. Do I believe that I *will* be with Pam again after my life ends? Yes, I do. In fact, I contacted two different mediums in 2020, and both gave me positive feedback along these lines. I hope they're right, and I hope that my faith is well placed here.

The other side of the coin has to do with the perfect length of my life. I still have many things to do. So, I'm trying to find a way for my grief to be fully in my bones while still embracing the joys of living life. That's a challenging balance to strike, but I'm committed to it.

I know that significant growth, healing, and evolution continue to occur. I get a vote on who the new John will be and what will be my new identity as a single person. I'm pursuing this new version with a healthy dose of curiosity, intent, and confidence. I know that I want to honor Pam and my parents in the choices I make while bringing this new guy out for the world to see. I want to live a full life, and Zuba's message strongly aligns with this kind of intention.

I'm also encouraged to look backward with gratitude in my head and in my heart. I've had incredibly good fortune in my life, and that starts with the fact that Pam chose me at all. I was in a relationship with her for forty-seven years, and I was her husband for thirty-nine years. I loved her with my full heart, and I know she felt the same way. How lucky was I to be *that guy* for so long—to have all those years with her by my side? The pain is now joined by the consistent and deeply felt gratitude for my life as her husband. This shift of perception puts me on a firmer foundation going forward. I don't think I could have done this when I first read *Permission to Mourn*. But I can do it now, and I'm glad that I picked it up and read it for a second time with new eyes.

The next book that stuck with me was Brené Brown's *Rising Strong*. She made a couple of points that had a significant influence on decisions I would make going forward. One of those was to simply strive to be kind to myself. I don't think that I was overly unkind to myself, but the question that I was encouraged to ask myself on a regular basis—and that is still written on the whiteboard in my laundry room—was, *What would kindness to myself look like today?* This gave me food for thought. It also shifted my brain away from what I'd lost, at least for a little while, to what I could do right now. I found myself going easier on the internal chatter and making some decent decisions about how I spent my time in this totally unfamiliar and solitary space.

However, the most powerful concept that Brown delivered was an aspirational one. I still use this on an almost daily basis. It's a conscious intent on my part to view people's actions—or lack thereof—by assuming that *they're doing the best that they can.*

For many months after losing Pam, I felt a white-hot anger. My perception that my brother, sister, and numerous friends had disappeared fueled that anger. I was treated like a pariah by my neighbors, and I felt totally forgotten by many people who'd been important to Pam and me. This lack of understanding of what I was going through still haunts me, but many discussions on this topic with my grief counselor have helped me inch forward.

The anger presented most prominently in my brother. I was deeply hurt and permanently scarred by Pam's death. I had not received a phone call or any type of communication from my only brother in many months. Did he care about me at all? Did he have any idea of the pain I was experiencing and had to manage?

After stewing in my anger, I called him to let him know that I was bitterly disappointed in his lack of communication with me. This was a mistake on my part.

"Pete, do you realize how damaged I am from losing Pam? Do you care? Because I'm in great need of support and empathy at this juncture. This feels like an egregious omission on your part."

He replied, "I think that egregious is an overly aggressive term and that this accusation is way out of line, John."

We hung up with this issue unresolved.

Looking back, I see that there was a pressure relief valve within me that needed to be released. I also felt that I needed to state my point of view.

I finally started to make some progress with significant mediating assistance from my grief counselor. I could see that Pete was simply doing the best he could. He wasn't doing what I hoped he would in terms of supporting his damaged younger brother, but I realized that my hopes for that type of relationship were unreasonable. Whenever any anger or resentment toward him started to bubble up in my head or my heart, my new go-to reaction was to find a way to believe that he—or anyone else who had ignored me since losing Pam—was simply doing the best he or she could under the circumstances. This was a very big step in my process toward healing.

Exercising this new default attitude remains a primary strategy for me when managing occasional feelings of isolation. What I strive to do now is to be free of as many expectations as I can when communicating about how grief has changed me. I try to meet others where they are. And if I can't engage in the type of authentic or deep conversation that I would like,

I remind myself that they're simply doing the best they can. Furthermore, others continue to experience their own grief related to Pam's death. I'm not always successful in moving my head and my heart to this space, but when I am, I can soothe my emotions and maintain important relationships in my life. This is a big deal, and I continue to prioritize these choices and these behaviors as often as I can.

Everyone has grief in their lives. I still believe that the death of a spouse or a child is a particularly intense type of pain that's impossible to conceive until it happens to you. But there are many other types of grief, and I imagine that just about everyone has experienced one or more of these.

When I could finally wrap my head and heart around that concept, the next idea for me to ponder and embrace is what I'll call *benefit-of-the-doubt love*. This idea came to me on my back deck, and I was reminded of our dog, Karma, who we lost in 2013. There's a magnet on my refrigerator that states, "May I always be the kind of person that my dog thinks I am." There's some real wisdom in that statement. When I was able to parse these words, it boiled down to the concept of giving everyone the benefit of the doubt. Dogs are very good at this.

When Karma was in my life, she was a devoted and happy dog. In return, this brought me happiness because she was always very happy to see me. She would enthusiastically chase frisbees with me, and she loved going to our property in Donnelly, Idaho (aka Camp Chaos), and running around. She was well trained in terms of being friendly to strangers, but if someone showed up at Camp Chaos unannounced, she greeted them with forceful barking until we told her to stop. Then she was their best friend, with her tail furiously wagging. She brought joy to my heart on a regular basis and was truly a member of our family. She was the perfect manifestation of benefit-of-the-doubt love and remains the gold standard for my demeanor.

This became one of my primary behavioral goals moving forward. I don't always succeed, but I believe I'm getting better at delivering this type of benefit-of-the-doubt love. I also see it, feel it, and greatly appreciate it when this kind of love is given to me.

The last book of influence is *The Grace in Dying* by Kathleen Dowling Singh. In the middle of the book are a series of chapters that address the psycho-spiritual stages of dying. This is where I discovered some deep insights about a number of unknowns associated with Pam's final weeks. I think many readers are familiar with Elisabeth Kubler Ross's five stages of grief. As a refresher, they are denial, anger, bargaining, depression, and acceptance. I certainly revisited this after Pam died. Some of it felt accurate, while other parts didn't really resonate with my experiences.

The last time I heard Pam speak was in early July 2019, when she had a very fragile airway. That fragility and the inherent risk to her health and life were remedied when her head and neck surgeon placed the trach tube into her stoma. She could now breathe with a robust airway and without the threat of it unexpectedly closing at any moment. But she could no longer speak. We managed communication with the Boogie Board, but she couldn't use it in the last three weeks of her life. She had no way of communicating with me. What was she thinking? What was she feeling? What did she need? Not knowing was agonizing.

I continued to talk to her about my love for her, my admiration for her as a mother and an active citizen in our hometown. I tried to let her know I was there for the entirety and wouldn't leave her side until she went through that portal where I could not go. I meant it all. She was my true love, and I was going to do everything I could to support her and ease her transition. I always stood ready to address any pain or needs she had *right now*. The pain of these memories is still fresh, but I was able to suppress it in my attempts to be the best caregiver I could be.

Reading Singh's book about a year after Pam's death finally gave me a modicum of comfort in answering these questions about what was happening within Pam. The author was a hospice nurse and had been present for the moment of death for numerous patients. She compiled her notes and observations and then shared them in this book. Interestingly, all the stages of grief from Dr. Kubler Ross were contained in her *first* stage of dying. She called this stage Chaos. There were two other psycho-spiritual stages that came after, and she titled them *Surrender* and *Transcendence*. The overall message was that the patient was in the process of accepting that this was going to be the end of their life on Earth.

The next steps made for some challenging reading, but they described what Singh believed was happening as the individual began readying themselves for the coming transition. This had been briefly described to me by some of the hospice staff who had visited our home in October 2019. They knew I was befuddled and troubled by the limited communication from Pam. They said that even if Pam was sleeping a lot, there was significant spiritual work that she was doing at this time. I accepted this concept, although I admit that I never fully understood it or questioned them about more details. I simply could not have a rational conversation about the details of the dying process when it actively involved my wife. Eventually, reading this book meant I could contemplate some of what might have been engaging her thoughts, faith, and spiritual processes in those final silent weeks of Pam's life. She was doing her subtle inner work to let go and prepare for a higher realm.

I understood Pam's faith very well, which allowed me valuable insights into how she was likely engaging these other psycho-spiritual stages of dying as laid out by Singh. This was very deep stuff for my engineering-wired brain and was likely one of the primary triggers for the awakening of my right brain. It was also highly comforting because I finally seemed to have some notion of what Pam was thinking and feeling in those final weeks. Pam was acknowledging that her life was about to end and was experiencing some of what her new reality was going to be. There were many aspects of this described by Ms. Dowling Singh, and they are accurately captured in her naming these stages as Surrender and Transcendence. I believe that this was hard work for her and that it took a lot of her time in those final weeks to reach the point where she felt ready to depart this life. I had to sit with all of this for a long time, but it eventually allowed me to have some understanding and empathy for what Pam had experienced. I believe all the courage and strength that she'd shown in her battles with cancer were now being applied to the process of peacefully closing the final chapter of her life on Earth. That was seminal in allowing me to move forward. This book gave me some ideas that I could embrace about what had occurred within my communication-challenged wife as Halloween approached in 2019.

I'm a very different man now, and the process of change continues. My sadness over losing Pam has not diminished much, but I find it's more manageable now due to the new perspectives I've gained. Grief is very hard work, and I was not well prepared for what I had to do. These new perspectives explain a lot about how my right brain awakened as I was forced to deal with the loss of my true love.

Change will continue to occur. I don't get to define the pace of this journey, but I can learn a lot by simply paying attention to what I'm thinking and feeling as I go forward. This isn't easy, nor is it impossible. If I can do it, I believe others experiencing deep grief can too. The right half of my brain is indeed awakening as I move forward, and I'm very glad for the evolution. I miss Pam every day, but my story isn't finished, so I'll do what I can to embrace this gift of my fortunate life for as long as I can.

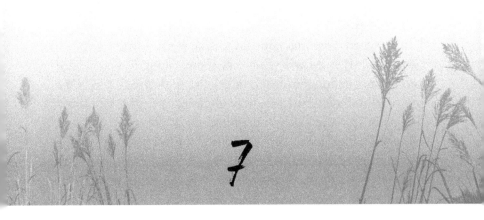

SERVICE AS AN EFFECTIVE SALVE

My life of community service began while Pam and I were young and early in parenthood. This was normally manifested as projects through our church. I remember one of my early pastors preached about serving God's kingdom here on Earth, and that sermon seemed to be aimed directly at me. Soon after, I joined the Missions and Outreach Committee at Hillview United Methodist Church (UMC) and formed some lifelong friendships through service opportunities to serve our hometown and our world.

The first project I remember participating in was the 1986 CROP Walk sponsored by Church World Service (CWS). This was held in October each year and was meant to align with World Hunger Day on the Christian calendar. It was a 10 km walk, and 75 percent of the proceeds went to CWS, and 25 percent went to the Idaho Foodbank Warehouse. I was motivated to see how many sponsors I could sign up, so

I approached potential contributors at work. I knew a ton of people at HP, and I was shameless about asking if they needed another tax deduction. I normally got a $20 pledge and had a pretty good feeling that we were all doing our part to address hunger in Treasure Valley and around the world. The Foodbank Warehouse had an excellent reputation for being run efficiently and serving numerous food pantries around Idaho. With this in mind, the 25 percent contribution was an effective pitch for a number of my sponsors.

That first year, I showed up with about $500 in sponsorships, and I was surprised to find out that I was among the top five fundraisers/walkers. I walked with our pastor, Jim, that day with our seven-month-old son, Geoff, in a backpack. Pastor Jim referenced me in his sermon the next Sunday and said that he felt compelled to do anything that needed to be done to make sure I made it to the finish line. My pledges were worth too much not to finish! I learned that service was highly satisfying and gave me enthusiastic joy.

That was the first of many projects that the Missions and Outreach committee provided me, and I got a real kick out of participating in other efforts. We shipped hospital beds to the country of Colombia and assembled a crew to get them ready for shipment. I helped arrange gatherings called SOFT, Sharing Our Faith Traditions, where representatives from various faith communities in the Treasure Valley gathered to discuss the nuts and bolts of our various theologies. There was bingo at the retirement home next to Hillview. And there was a monthly commitment to the El-Ada Soup Kitchen.

Pam and I embraced the soup kitchen work enthusiastically, and it became a regular family activity as Geoff and Jessica grew up. Some days, it involved cooking the meal. Often, we were part of the front-facing team that served the meal and interacted with the guests. And many times, I found myself in front of the industrial dishwasher in the El-Ada kitchen washing dishes. Pam and I had decided to get the kids involved with this kind of community service work when they were young, and this continued through their high school years, including hosting exchange students along the way. It was important to us that our children understood the abundance we enjoyed and that service to our neighbors was an important value in our family.

Perhaps even more interesting were my thoughts and feelings while serving in this manner. Many Sundays, we'd come home from worship, and I wasn't at all in the mood to run back to El Ada that afternoon. We'd made a commitment to serve, so I never seriously considered abrogating that agreement, but I still felt the annoyance factor. The epiphany was the consistency of how I felt *after* we'd served at the soup kitchen. The annoyance disappeared, and I was always glad (and proud) that we'd given our time to participate in this manner. When I stepped back and analyzed this sequence, I saw that service charged my batteries and, thus, was a component of the life I wanted to continue to pursue. In my more philosophical moments, I could also see that God was tweaking my nose in these circumstances and reminding me to *pay attention* and lean into the benefits of service work, especially when my wife and children were part of the crew.

After numerous years of projects with Hillview UMC, I felt a tug to explore service opportunities outside of the church. We hosted our first Rotary exchange student in 2002, and by 2008, we had hosted two more. I began to think that I should consider joining Rotary. I admired the work they did, and I enjoyed the company of these high-character individuals, so in the fall of 2009, I joined the Rotary Club of Boise Sunrise. I chose this club because they were a breakfast club meeting and met at 7:00 a.m. on Tuesdays. I could easily make those weekly meetings, whereas the demands of my job at HP meant that it would be difficult to make a weekly lunch meeting. I was surrounded by service-oriented individuals, and I quickly made a lot of new friends among this group of kindred spirits.

My first project with the club was delivering dictionaries (aka Gazetteers) to third graders at Taft Elementary School in Boise. The club supported these deliveries to six schools, and I was invited to join the merry band headed to Taft. We paid for these books, and one of the Rotary club members personalized each book with a student's name in calligraphy. There were a lot of refugee children at Taft, and I remember having to carefully sound out some of the names in my head before I called them up to get their new and personalized Gazetteer. The lead Rotarian that day made a brief speech about how important reading and literacy were and said that our service club had chosen *these students* as our service project that day. We were putting our money where our mouths were, and he asked them to use the book each day to learn a new word and expand their vocabulary. I took good notes, and the next year, I became the lead Rotarian to deliver dictionaries to a different school. I still serve in this manner on an annual basis. Our Rotary club now delivers to twelve schools—a delightful project in support of youth and literacy.

The real work was yet to come as I was asked to be part of District 5400—southern Idaho—Rotary Youth Exchange (RYE) committee. The district had a strong student exchange program in place already, and we usually had anywhere from fourteen to twenty-four students on the move each year. The "inbounds" were the foreign students coming to Idaho, and the "outbounds" were Idaho teenagers headed overseas. We arranged one-for-one exchanges in both directions. I learned a lot and mentored several foreign teenagers who spent a full school year in Idaho or abroad. We normally found them three host families, so each family had the student in their homes for fifteen to eighteen weeks. Pam and I had already hosted three times (we would do it once more), so I had some experience that helped me get rolling when the work needed to be addressed. There was an enormous amount of paperwork that we were required to manage for Rotary International (RI) and for the US Department of State. I expanded my network of Rotary contacts quite extensively and eventually became the Inbound Coordinator and then the Committee Chairman—all rewarding experiences.

At the end of my chairmanship for Rotary Youth Exchange, Pam's health took a turn for the worse. I had assembled a high-performance RYE committee by this time, so the work got done while I was busy elsewhere. At this time, I was also the Chairman of the Board at Semilla Nueva, the NGO in Guatemala working on bio-fortified corn.

My service work shifted into neutral while I focused on being the best caregiver for Pam. I essentially disappeared from these positions when we went into hospice in September 2019. My disappearing act did not end with her death on Halloween.

In early grief, my brain was working at a diminished capacity, and my heart was thoroughly broken. We had a memorial service for Pam on December 7, 2019. When everyone left to go home, I found myself in a very quiet house, overwhelmed by everything that was my new reality. I had no idea how to engage everything in front of me now that my familiar life had been blown to smithereens.

Eventually, in early 2020, my rational thought began to return, and I wondered if going back to service projects might be a good idea. It was an easy decision to include service as part of my new life, but I didn't have a clear idea about what I wanted to do. I did my best to pay attention, which led me to the conclusion that I had abundant freedom to choose many of the aspects of who this new guy was going to be. I re-upped for another term on the Semilla Nueva board (I was to be assigned as the secretary as a new chairman had been installed), and I closed out my chairmanship of the Youth

Exchange Committee for D5400. I had an excellent successor already identified, so that transition went quite smoothly. I was nominated to become the president of the Rotary Club of Boise Sunrise, which is a multi-year process. My presidential year would be 2022–2023, so on July 1, I became the president-nominee.

Yes, these projects were effective distractions from my pain, but they were very good distractions. I love being involved in service where significant impact is involved. Semilla Nueva is a perfect example. We'd gone through a lot of interesting chapters in our attempts to effectively address chronic malnutrition in Guatemala. As of early 2020, we had our first bio-fortified corn seed on the market, and it was branded Fortaleza 3 or F3. Fortaleza means strength, and we had a new sales and marketing director in place. Angela was going to take the company down the path of competing for market share with low- to medium-acreage farmers in Guatemala with F3. This was to be a market-based solution where we appealed to farmers (not end-user corn consumers), and our value proposition was based on low-cost seeds that delivered high yields and were drought resistant. Consumer preference studies showed that F3 was a corn variant that also delivered a tastier and softer tortilla.

At that time, I was the only one on the board who came from a large company. As the corporate guy on the board, I had experience in competing and fighting for market share with what we believed was a superior product. Therefore, I had a unique voice in many of the board discussions about how we would succeed in this new commercial venture.

This was the first time (that we knew of) that this kind of project had been developed using a market-based approach. We'd made our fair share of mistakes along the way, but we felt that we were pursuing the right model with the right staffing. And it was an excellent distraction for my broken heart. The project had the potential of benefitting hundreds of thousands of lives in the short term and up to a billion lives in the long term. The promise of what bio-fortified crops could deliver was intoxicating for me as an avowed impact junkie. I strove to inject a couple catchy tag lines into the board meetings along the lines of "Let's go change the world" and "Let's go improve the diets of an entire country." This was my kind of work, and it helped put me back together in the early days of my grief journey.

I expect that service will continue to be part of my life because I very clearly see that my time on this earth is finite and limited, and I want to serve while I still can. I want to leave this life better than I found it. I want to shine a bright light on the fact that this is how we build our personal legacies. How we behave and what we support are the building blocks of our legacies—something not to be taken lightly.

I still have a long way to go in this process. I'm not sure what's going to happen in the future, but I strive to pay attention and keep my eyes, ears, and heart open, so I can notice the terrific people and circumstances around me. I will never forget Pam. She will be with me every day until the end of my life. My faith assures me that we will unite again. But I'm not meant to simply take up space. I have gifts to offer, and I can, indeed, leave life better than I found it. Service will be a significant part of the rest of my story; it's a salve on my broken heart.

ACCEPTANCE AND THE SERENITY PRAYER

As I sat on my back deck and pondered what would come next, I boiled it down to two primary categories. The first was inventing and configuring a new life, which meant envisioning what I wanted to do with the rest of my life. The second was to find acceptance of Pam's death. I've made significant progress in the first category. The second moves forward at an extremely slow pace. I don't get to choose the pace that emanates from the unconscious.

First, I had to get used to living alone. I hadn't lived without a roommate or spouse for at least forty years. My grief counselor asked if I was comfortable in my house, and the answer was an easy, "Yes." She was surprised because she'd had other clients who couldn't stay in the house they'd shared with their departed spouses. Fortunately, that was not the case for me. I was comfortable in my space, which had been our space. My son and his wife were concerned about my being alone and suggested that I get a puppy. I inherently trust these two impressive young adults, so I gave it a lot of thought. But I valued my freedom, and the puppy never made it into the picture.

My identity as husband and as the old John was gone forever. Change was coming, and I was curious about how much I could influence the process. There were surprises along the way, but I believed that I could direct much of the change that would define my new life. This felt empowering in the face of bitter loss.

Pam and I were recovering alcoholics, and we both got sober in 2011. She made that choice in July, and I joined her in saying goodbye to alcohol in October. The Serenity Prayer is invaluable to recovering alcoholics. An excerpt of that powerful prayer from Reinhold Neibuhr follows:

> *God, grant me the serenity to accept the things I cannot change*
> *The courage to change the things I can*
> *And the wisdom to know the difference.*

Acceptance of the permanence of Pam's absence was a challenging goal after forty-seven years. I'm moving toward this very slowly. There are still parts of me that ask, "How could this have happened?!" It's rarely ever a question of *why* it happened. I don't know if my left-brain nature is afoot here, but it's curious that it always seems to present as the *how* question.

Acceptance would put me on more solid ground because I'd recognize that this new reality is permanent, even though it's the deepest anathema to the longing of my heart and soul. What I do know is that a *lack* of acceptance of Pam's death is not acceptable. So, I have work to do. I get glimpses of what this might look like, and these often come after talking to other widows and widowers. We don't even need to speak about our absent spouses. It's enough to be in conversation with someone who's also experienced this searing pain and grief. For some set of reasons, these conversations seem to move me just a little closer toward acceptance. It's still a long way off, but I know it's a goal worth pursuing.

On my darker days, I assert that it will *never* be OK that Pam died. In the next breath, I also acknowledge that I cannot change this fact. My grief has become more manageable and more understandable with time, but the concept of acceptance still seems far away. I also recognize that the passage of time can deliver wisdom and perspective, but it doesn't guarantee the delivery of acceptance.

Lately, I've found some interesting evidence of acceptance creeping into my thoughts. The best way to describe it is that it seems to be coming to me in layers. I can find acceptance in portions of my current life, which also means that I can see and accept that other parts of my life aren't coming back. I'm encouraged by this kind of progress, but at the same time, I see a more realistic picture of what acceptance will look like. I don't think I'll ever fully accept certain parts of the overall picture, but I might be quite off target on that assertion. In the aggregate, this is a very interesting process that seems to be *happening to me*. I bring intent to this scenario, but it's more about simply paying attention, which primarily includes naming and identifying my feelings. But I also need to listen to friends and trusted individuals. I'm not sure what I expected this process to look like, but it's turning out to be quite different from what I thought.

Simply paying attention to my head and heart and to others around me supports this objective. Other than that, I'm not in control of much of this process. I just need to roll with it and its chosen pace. I believe I'll get there. As time goes by, I think my conscious and unconscious psyches are being rewired without Pam's presence. I strive to reach her in a spiritual, not physical, realm. Sometimes, I believe that Pam is never gone. Other times, I struggle with thoughts of her being gone forever since I can't see or touch her. Slowly, I move toward acceptance that she and I will not create new memories. While this can cause short-lived pain, it also nudges me to remember and cherish our memories together.

Many months after my loss, I began to see my personal grief process more clearly. In short, I had to figure out how I grieved. I knew that everyone engaged in grief in their own way. That was easy to learn and internalize. But I needed to keep doing the work and then take a step back and understand what *my process of grieving* involved. This wasn't simple because self-evaluation is never objective. I needed to wrap my arms around this, so I had a more concrete idea of who I was and where I was headed.

The first piece was that I admitted to myself that I would always, to the end of my days, lead with my head. As the theme of this book indicates, I was experiencing an authentic awakening of my right brain and heart. This has taken a long time to acknowledge and understand. When I was able to take that step of self-examination and see myself as clearly as I could, it was obvious that my journey of wrestling with and processing my grief always started with my head. Leading with my head means that my way of experiencing the world is to observe, analyze, and exist in the world of ideas and perceptions. Eventually, I'm able to bring my heart into this process, and I then feel and acknowledge my emotions.

As I looked back on our entire experience with cancer, I realized how much we both had *been told what to do* in terms of therapies that had the greatest chance of success. We had ceded control to numerous outstanding and brilliant healthcare professionals in an attempt to bring the finest counterattack to our battle against this disease. This lack of control became clearest when we went into hospice in September 2019. The disease was now progressing at a very rapid rate, and in the end, I had no control over losing Pam. I could see physical changes in her, but the hospice nurses helped me accurately interpret what was happening.

The primary nurse on Pam's hospice team said, "John, you don't need to continue the rigorous feeding schedule for Pam at this point. All that's being fed now is further tumor growth."

This brought me to my knees. "I'm supposed to stop feeding her! How can that be a good idea?"

I broke down and cried uncontrollably as those words sunk in. Pam was very close to death, and my role as caregiver was to adopt this new set of guidelines. Even that level of control had been removed from me/us, which contributed to my shattered self-esteem as the end of Pam's life drew near. I was forced—as an alpha male—to accept an undeniable surrender of control. My faith did *not* provide me comfort at that time.

When I pondered my new life after Pam's death, I recognized that I wanted to regain some level of control over what happened and what would be next. Simultaneously, I needed to find a way to understand what had happened to *my life* and how all those dreams had been derailed by a heartless disease that had effectively detonated all my plans. I knew that accepting Pam's death was a crucial component going forward, and I was under no illusions that this was going to happen easily or on any schedule that I might define. The destination was clear; the process, schedule, and the learnings were not clear at all.

Months and months later, the forward-looking intent remained at the top of my mind because I now had an unexpected and yet intoxicating freedom in my life. I knew what I wanted (understanding, acceptance, control), and I vaguely recognized that I had the power to make these things come to pass. I would take these decisions one at a time.

I expect to change and learn a lot along the way, and this conception brings me back to the importance of paying attention all the time. I'm called to figure out what I'm supposed to learn along the way and to experience the whole thing. Accepting Pam's death must eventually happen because, aligned with the Serenity Prayer, it's something I cannot change. I believe I will approach this goal in a somewhat asymptotic (nice engineering term, eh?) manner and that it will be with me for the rest of my life. There's some comfort in this knowledge, and it reminds me to be patient and vigilant along this path.

GRIEVING DURING
A PANDEMIC

The COVID-19 pandemic hit the United States four months after Pam died. I'd already started my grief journey in several ways, but this event was to prove both challenging and instructional. From March 2020 until I got my first vaccine in March 2021, there was palpable fear everywhere. Infections were spreading quickly, followed by death rates that were grim and startling. How could this have happened? Or, in my more rational moments, I thought, *How did it take so long for something like this to hit us?* I had a lot of alone time and, thus, had some decisions to make.

Philosophically, I was stunned at how the pandemic became politicized. It was reminiscent of what I'd thought and hoped would occur with climate change challenges versus what actually happened. We had a foe that didn't care about sovereign borders or political ideology. It wanted to replicate itself as efficiently as it could, and if that meant killing off large numbers of humans, so be it. I thought we'd pull together and fight this scourge. Wrong again! Instead, there were loud protests over masks, school closings, social distancing, and the general inconvenience caused by this virus.

After watching the news, I formed some conclusions about how I would frame my decisions. It boiled down to making a commitment about how I thought, acted, and spoke. I consciously committed myself to the goal of looking back at some point in the future and being proud of the guy I was during these difficult times.

I had some ideas about how I'd endure this isolation. I had my musical instruments and a new room that I devoted to music. I played my trombone and my bass guitar, and I continued to read. With my understanding of social distancing and the nature of how the virus could spread, I felt comfortable getting on my bike, hitting a bucket of golf balls, or taking a walk to calm my brain in a pandemic-compliant manner. My sister Beth in Chicago was literally stuck in her condo for weeks at a time, so I felt grateful to live in Boise and be able to pursue my chosen activities.

I drew another conclusion that was a bit further afield. I came to see the earth as a living organism as opposed to a volcanic rock. Literature of old often called this Pangaea. After pondering what we humans had done—and continue to do—to damage the planet we all call home, I started believing that Pangaea had chosen this time to unleash a particularly nasty virus as a pushback against the homo sapiens who were doing so much atmospheric damage. I still believe this to be the case.

I stayed at home and waited for the development of a vaccine to combat this nasty bug. This gave me a lot of time to think about Pam and her absence. I was learning a lot from my grief-related reading, and my physical fitness was improving. But I was still heartbroken without Pam by my side.

Early in the pandemic, I realized I was glad that Pam wasn't part of this scenario. At the end of her life, she was significantly immune-compromised, and there was a high-touch theme with everyone from hospice when they visited her during her final six weeks. I had some occasional bereavement contact with the hospice team in 2020, and I asked them about their high-touch approach during a global pandemic. I wasn't surprised when they told me that this had been abandoned. That one detail would have dramatically changed our hospice experience in a negative manner. I began to see examples of small things for which I could be grateful. Although I missed her terribly every day, part of me was glad that she wasn't part of the pandemic trainwreck.

I further internalized what Brené Brown said about everyone doing the best they could. I chose to consciously adopt a universal benefit-of-the-doubt attitude in a more comprehensive manner. It was a unique time in the history of the United States when we all experienced significant and chronic stress. My parents taught me that one's true nature emerges under significant stress. My dad had been deployed to the Philippines during WWII, and both my parents had experienced chronic stress during those years. What kind of character would I demonstrate under this current stress?

With this as a frame, I saw the pandemic as an opportunity to reinvent myself, as well as to pay attention and closely observe what was going on around me. How was I going to behave? What kind of stress-triggered behavior might I see in others? This attitude served to mold me into who I was going to be while a widespread illness wrote this chapter of our nation's history.

I listened and learned as much as I could to tilt the odds in my favor of not getting infected. I purchased a small rechargeable electric fan to use if I went to a restaurant. A little airflow could prevent an airborne virus from lingering near me and entering my system.

Our weekly Rotary meetings met virtually, and while that went well, I missed the company of these friends. I headed up the grants committee at Boise Sunrise, and our primary fundraiser was an event called Lobsterfest. I'd missed the 2019 event while Pam was so ill, and because I would soon be the club president, it was my job to figure out who would get the $35,000 we'd raised at the event. I decided how we would proceed, which was largely supported—but also energetically discussed—among club members who thought it was a less-than-ideal approach to this distribution task. We had a healthy number of grant applications, and we had the freedom to make grants from $500 and up to $5,000 to 501(c)(3) non-profit organizations all over the Treasure Valley. The pandemic had hit these organizations universally hard, and many of them were simply trying to figure out how to keep their doors open. That made my decision easy. Everyone would get a check this year. We could talk about how much to donate to each organization, but the basic theme was if an organization had taken the time to submit an application for a grant, they'd get a check this year. Good idea? I thought so, and I effectively sold it, and this was how we distributed grants in 2020. My responsibility in leading this task was satisfying, and it decreased the lonely isolation of the pandemic.

Furthermore, I realized that I needed to take personal ownership of telling the stories about the projects we supported at Boise Sunrise. Prior to that year, the checks were dropped in the mail with a nice letter from the club president. That was not how that year's checks were going to be distributed. I invited various club members to personally deliver the checks, and a few individuals took me up on this invitation. Socially distanced and fully masked, I ended up delivering about half of them myself to an after-school STEM program, the Idaho Diaper Bank, the Girl Scouts, a charter school, and a couple of agencies serving homeless clients. I had a ball. This was more fun than anyone should be allowed to have—especially during a pandemic.

The Idaho Diaper Bank is committed to helping low-income new parents have access to diapers for their new baby. They have a storage space filled with pallets of diapers, and they were having a staff meeting when I swung by with the grant check. They put in countless hours negotiating low prices for diapers and then managing significant logistics in obtaining and storing them before distributing them to the families they served. I was mightily impressed with their efforts and told them that we were proud to be able to support this compassionate and challenging work. I loved meeting them and seeing the hard work they were doing to make a real difference in the lives of numerous families. This was a perfect example of our efforts to leave it better than we found it!

I asked for a picture with each non-profit's representative, and I chatted them up about what they were doing and how they planned to use the donated funds. I can't tell you how delightful it was to hear about the work they were already doing and what our funds would enable. Those photos and stories were then posted on the Rotary club's website. Again, this was a very effective antidote for COVID isolation.

I believe that everyone has had a chance to rub shoulders with grief due to this pandemic. Many of us lost family members or friends, and all of us lost tangible components of our chosen lifestyle. The pandemic helped me to see that there is grief in every life, and this was subtle but critical learning for me. While I still believe that there's an island of deep grief populated by those who have lost a child or a spouse, I also see that we all walk around with some level of grief in our bones and our hearts. The COVID-19 virus delivered new manifestations of grief while simultaneously shining a brighter light on existing grief while we were isolated.

I feel at peace regarding my good fortune as well as the integrity of my choices during this time. Two of the foundational pillars that got me through the hospice experience and the months since I lost Pam were striving to be in the moment right now and to seek gratitude where I could. The pandemic was an accelerator in moving those choices forward and keeping them top of mind. I continue to change, and I still strive to pay attention and demonstrate resilience. I also seek to deliver the benefit-of-the-doubt love and kindness to all. These guidelines will continue to be my behavioral guardrails going forward.

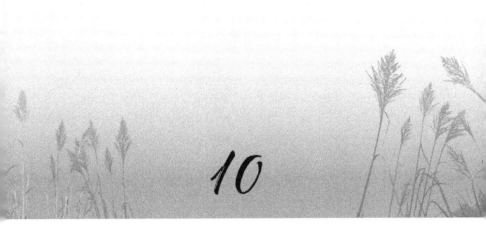

EXPRESSING GRIEF THROUGH POETRY

The summer of 2020 was still my first year of grief, which meant that everything was a first for me without Pam. Our wedding anniversary, Pam's birthday, Christmas, the anniversary of the date we met. You get the idea. I did my best to engage each of these with my eyes, ears, and heart wide open. What was this one going to feel like? How could I invite pain to join me on another first?

This was instructive, challenging, and at times, infuriating. All my efforts didn't remove the fifty-ton weight that always sat on my chest. My anger and a seemingly bottomless well of deep grief didn't seem to be going anywhere. Within all of this, I believe my mental circuit breakers began to kick back in. They did this at random times and at their own pace. It was up to me to simply pay attention and notice when interesting thoughts and feelings presented themselves.

I wondered how I might capture some of these mini epiphanies. There seemed to be a series of significant things bubbling up. I'm not sure how the next idea came to me, but in June 2020, I scratched out my first poem to capture what I was feeling. It's still one of my favorites from about sixteen poems I wrote.

My World Now

Thoughts of you come to me at random times
Or do I invite them to come?
I see us in many of our shared adventures
I look back because I do not know how to look forward with you

I harbor many hopes about you and your current status
I hope you are pain free
I hope you are safe and secure
I hope you are surrounded by love
I hope you are in the company of loved ones who have gone on before you
How do I turn hope into faith?

Faith remains to me, believing in things unseen and unheard
I cannot see you now though I wish I could
I cannot hear you, but I desperately hope that can change
Is my faith strong enough to truly believe all that I hope for you?
Is the bottom line of this process really a test of faith for me?
It feels like this is where I am headed

I am told how lucky I was to have this life with you
I hear it, and yet it is not penetrating my psyche with any urgency
I wonder about it getting into my head
And more importantly into my heart
The pace will be different for those two destinations

All of this moves at its own pace
Which is fundamentally unfamiliar to me
I am asked to remain present and to pay attention as my role in
this process
I do this as well as I can
And I strive to bring gratitude to the entire experience

For I have been extraordinarily lucky to have loved you
And to have been loved by you
To join together to experience adventures
To learn how to be a good parent
And to work as a team to leave it better than we found it

When I can embrace the present moment
And acknowledge the significant good fortune in my life
I can begin to see what eventual acceptance looks like
I am far from accepting this disaster
I still scream and rail at the Almighty
And the walls in the house we shared
But I can begin to see glimpses of where this all goes

I love you, and I will always love you
You were truly the one for me
I was lucky to have had all this time with you
And any backward glances need to acknowledge that good fortune
I will move forward with grief and loss
And you will always be with me

What will it be like to look forward?
Who shall I become without you at my side?
How can I make you proud of the man I am—the man I will be?
How could this have happened?
How will I learn to accept this?
Will my faith get me through?
Are you well, my love?
I miss you so

My initial reaction was interesting. It was an unkind minimization of what I was doing. What kind of crap would come out of a heartbroken engineer who hadn't dusted off his creative writing skills in a very long time? Who would ever want to read this stuff? Soon after confronting these foolish and misguided thoughts, I was reminded that it was a good idea for me to find ways to be kind to myself. So, I did some editing on my first draft and started a file folder entitled Poetry Musings. I shared some of these with close friends but not very widely. Interestingly enough, I kept at it for another nine weeks.

Another memorable poem came to me a few days later. I actually found myself running in from my back deck to my laptop, so I could capture what was running through my head. The thought that triggered all of this was one that I'd shared with my grief counselor a little later. It was along the lines of what it might have been like if I had died first, and Pam was the one left alone on the back deck, managing her grief.

What If the Roles Had Been Reversed?

I battled the beast first
It wasn't clear what that outcome was to be
And Pam was still cancer free that fall
What would reversed positions look like if things had unfolded differently?

What would I want for my true love left behind?
A path to a new form of happiness
Progress through this fog and morass
An eventual acceptance of what cannot be made right

What might she wonder about me?
What would her world here look like with me out of the picture?
I think I know some of what that would be like
We were true soulmates

From that perspective, what might I learn now?
Change is afoot and growth is apparent
New questions are being asked by me
About me

What shall looking forward alone be like?
What personal goals might be aligned with the process I am riding?
Can I trust all of this?
I must trust all of this and keep my eyes and ears and heart open
to what is in front of me
I am here
I wish you were as well

I didn't see this—my desire to write poetry—coming. In retrospect, there were a number of things at work. I wanted to find a way to capture what I was thinking and experiencing. I felt a curious level of freedom because I was so completely off balance in trying to do the things that my grief counselor had encouraged in terms of embracing pain and putting myself squarely into the arena with overwhelming grief. Writing did make me feel better. I was hesitant about with whom I might share this vulnerable space.

This next poem contains an interesting set of thoughts that I pondered. I was feeling the passage of time since the last time I saw and communicated with Pam. Memories took on fewer of the painful and sharp edges by then, but it was also painfully apparent that my life was moving on without Pam at my side. I wondered if I really did want healing to occur when I considered the trade-off.

Do I Want Everything to Heal?

I find myself pondering healing
While I also reflect on the life we shared.
Healing comes with time and introspection.
More time away from losing you
Seems to translate to more healing in me.
And so, I find that I do not want
Everything to heal in me.

The sharp stabs of this loss
Are less intense with time,
And I will accept and welcome this type of healing.
But this factor of time also becomes
A clear marker of how long we have been separated,
And from that frame, I do not wish for more healing.

I can see that the space I am in now
Allows me to kick open some interesting
And unexpected doors of opportunity.
This intrigues me.
What shall be next for me?

My bones and my heart are now beginning
To accept and understand and absorb this pain.
I know that you will be with me forever now.
This is a pleasant epiphany.
Yet it comes with questions
Of how I might have this grief
Coexist with a desire to live a full life.

You were indeed all that I wanted,
And there is an enormous blessing contained therein.
I created my life with you at my side,
And I was a very lucky man to have that option.

I remain in a slowly shrinking sense of disbelief
That you are gone from my sight.
I will look closer into my heart and my memories,
And I will continue to find you in there
Smiling and laughing and loving me
As your own true love.

You will always be that true love for me
Regardless of how much healing occurs
In my head and in my heart.

As I thought about the freedom of my future, the following poem emerged. While I had the challenges of learning to live alone and managing the sadness of not having Pam with me, there was also a new level of freedom that was appealing and almost intoxicating. I had a long conversation with my daughter about that, and she gave me some great feedback. The conversation was unlike any that I'd ever had in my life, and it's reflected in the content of this poem.

What I See Ahead

As I noodle on my own future
I can begin to see distant glimpses
Of a general destination for me.
The path ahead and behind
Is anything but direct and straight,
And this is indeed an interesting journey.

There is unique opportunity in front of me
To define and create this new fellow.
And establishing goals for this adventure
Sounds correct and very appealing to me.

While there is a long way to go here
Some of the details begin to snap into clearer focus.
Simply sitting still and pondering these
Appears to be a good start for now.

What does this look like?
That goals list is headed by **achieving full acceptance**
Of the disaster of last Halloween.
That is a complicated and multilayered objective
That is far, far away right now.

There are multiple components
Of striving **to practice freely given forgiveness,**
Which will shape this new guy
In important and foundational ways.

My old friends of **gratitude**
And **being fully present in the moment**
Will certainly continue to play very prominent roles
In the decision-making processes being developed
In my head and in my heart.

A recent addition which seems to be crucial
Is related to my attempts
In **meeting people where they are at**.
This one will be a bit tricky, I fear,
But the desired payoff in deeper personal relations
Seems to be calling for this development effort.

One clear member of this menu
Of desired personal traits and behaviors in the new me
Is to blow as many expectations
To smithereens as possible.
I will strive for maximum shrapnel and devastation
Relating to the destruction of these expectations.
As opposed to any persistent survivors in this obsolete category.

Numerous trusted sources and authors
Have emphasized the critical importance
Of me finding ways
To be consistently kind to myself.
I can agree with this, and it is well with my heart.
Yet I am occasionally less than kind.
Now I seek to lean into these episodes
And then confront myself on this onerous behavior
And shift it back to kindness.
It is time to say goodbye to unkindness to myself, I think.

The term **"benefit-of-the-doubt love"**
Keeps coming up in my thoughts.
Another concept that I wish to embody
Is represented by the word **"authenticity."**
What will these fundamental goals look like?
That is a question that I am intensely interested
In answering as part of this whole process.

How might I wish to be referred to in the future?
Evolved is one term of interest.
Empathy seems to be slowly emerging here.
And I have always admired really **good listeners**.

One reminder that will have immediate effects
Is the simple mantra of
Don't Take it Personally!
This sounds like it might feed
Some of the other goals
And is simple to remember
Yet challenging to deliver.

I remain grounded in optimism for my future.
I react well when I take the time to think
And to set worthy goals
For something this important.

Love shall be the bottom line here, I believe.
Now I will set out to figure out
What this looks and sounds like
To me and to others around me.

This is gonna take a while.

How patient was I in demanding my friends be with me as I processed my grief? How much of a pain in the ass was my demeanor? The answer seemed to be highly related to who I might be talking about, as some friends gave me a lot of space and still strove to keep in touch, while others disappeared. It was a mild cry for help, and the message was, *Hang in here with me, please. I think I can figure this out, but it's going to take time.*

Don't Lose Faith in Me

Do I believe I can navigate this process?
The title above is more about me believing in ME
Than about anyone else maybe losing faith in me
In the spirit of striving to be kind to myself
I will endeavor to not/never lose faith in me.

I did lose faith in the last months.
Not faith in me
But faith in terms of an event that can't be made right
Landing in my life and exploding that life
Blowing my beliefs off their foundation
Only to be considered much later

I can describe my hopes
But the picture around faith remains fuzzy in many ways
I lost my faith on many layers
But I am in the process of finding it again
I know I will see it with new eyes

If I can find ways to be consistently kind to myself
Then this action should put me on a solid foundation going forward
If I can be consistently authentic
And strive to meet others where they are
Then I think I can retain my faith in me

The bigger picture of where this is all headed
Seems to be coming into focus, oh so slowly
Gratitude and forgiveness and love and acceptance
All play significant roles in this picture
I wish I could share this with you
But it was your departure that started this process

I had all that I wanted in loving you
And parts of me remained unexamined
Or underdeveloped because of that
I will always miss those times
Along with missing you so desperately

But that is not my new reality
And thus I am moving into uncharted territory
What will this new life hold for me?
And what is that new John going to look like?

I will hold onto faith in myself
And see this through
To the best of my ability
I hope to see you again someday
You were the one for me

This next poem addresses a direct set of questions about
my mental circuit breakers coming back online. I hadn't yet
figured out the metaphor until I had this epiphany about part
of me dying when Pam died. I wondered what else was no
longer a part of me after the disastrous loss of my lifelong love.
I still wonder about this now. What should be jettisoned, and

what should be retained? What does that new guy look like, and how does he behave?

What Is Gone

Part of me died on Halloween,
But I am just recognizing this foggy space now.
What took so long?
What course corrections are now called for?
With this surprising new clarity,

What does permanently losing part of me look like?
Perhaps much more importantly,
What does that FEEL like?
Will I be up to the task to clearly see this
For ALL of what it really is?

Memories are a source of comfort,
But that deceased status is not materially altered.
At the most basic level,
What will I discover
As something that I must say goodbye to?

And how might I grieve something like this?
Maybe I've had some practice already.
In going toe to toe with the beast myself
And in finally jettisoning ethanol from my life.
Perhaps I have a bit of precedence
That I can lean into moving forward.

But the bottom line relating to this flash
Is that I must seek and then clearly see
That tangible parts of me are no longer in the picture.

With time and patience,
I intend to understand these departures.
And to seek peace and acceptance
Of this new reality.
I will tip my hat to those dead parts
And recognize them for what they meant to me
And for what they were in my life.

I wonder what I am going to find here.

I wanted to include this last poem to share how far afield
my thoughts were taking me in the summer of 2020. There
is clearly a healthy component of anger. It took the form of
me sneering at the universe: "You took my wife. I'm still here,
asshole. Is that all you got?" I've tried to avoid remaining in
that space of anger, but it still shows up. I'm not afraid of death
anymore. This poem had me baring my teeth to some entity
and aggressively stating that, while large parts of my world had
crumbled around me, I was still standing.

That Bullseye Shot That Rocked Me

Losing my beloved wife to a relentless disease
Is felt by me as a direct hit of an anti-aircraft missile.
That explosion found its mark
In detonating my life and shattering my heart.

What else might now eclipse such a blow?
Nothing, methinks.
So, I look back at "the universe" differently now.
There are critical times in my life at this point
Where I feel a specific question slither into my brain.
"Is that all you have?"
I am still here, pal.

How to describe such a stance?
Insouciance is a term that comes to mind,
Or maybe resilience.
Certainly, FREEDOM is now on this menu for me.
I have absorbed the shot,
And that delivered some unexpected liberation
For my head and my heart.

This comes with a visual component from my face.
It is best described as a subtle SCOWL
That also contains a full dose of complete commitment.
A slightly menacing visage in reaction to this hammer blow.
A look that might make a "paying attention" bystander
Take a step back and wonder, *What is up with that guy?*

It is not a great idea to embrace anger on a regular basis,
But it is equally foolish to ignore this coping tactic.
I am not fully freed of the deep rage-like feeling
That the most important person in my life
Was taken from me prematurely.
Yet, I feel this scowl has its place
Among the panoply of emotions
That I now get to actively manage.

I move forward to the best of my ability.
I have many new ideas as goals
While I seek to find acceptance and understanding of this disaster.
I am "all in" to do this challenging work,
And I can now see that a small part of it
Comes with a powerful and intriguing scowl.

It's interesting to go back and read these now, eighteen
months later. I'm not that guy anymore, but I clearly remember being in that unfamiliar space. My poetry was part of my
early journey, and I was surprised when it showed up. Being
open to what was happening in my brain and in my heart was

the starting point. Simply paying attention. And then writing it down in a manner that seemed to make sense at the time. This was a curious side road on the path of grief for me.

And now I ask you, "What interesting detour might you allow yourself to make to come to a better understanding of all the new and un-ignorable things that are happening to you on your unique journey?"

WHY AM I STILL HERE?

The question, "Why am I still here?" has risen frequently since Pam died, and I think I'm beginning to understand a few of the reasons. I needed to achieve a level of perspective to even ask this question and to be in a position to conceive and explore some answers. A lot had to happen before I could consider the question of why I'm still here.

The best way to begin is to state some of my basic beliefs. I think that we, as humans who wish to thrive and grow, are at our best when we're reaching for something just beyond our current grasp. When we're striving toward impactful and achievable goals, I think we're in a very good space.

That belief aligned well with the meritocracy at HP that defined how I was paid. Part of my work called for clear communications, and I found I was pretty good at this. Similarly, engineers were held in high esteem at HP, so I often found myself in a position to mentor others in this job. That was not something to be approached lightly. Done correctly, a colleague can grow and succeed in their career with well-targeted mentoring, and I was a recipient of this many times. In short, I took the mentorship gig very seriously and did my homework whenever I recognized that this was part of meeting my documented objectives.

From a high-level point of view, I saw myself as a problem solver. This was good because I liked solving problems. I was also competitive, and this was a valued trait at HP, so I leaned into these understandings. I wanted to be the guy who was chosen to address the nastiest and most impact-potential problems that faced my department. This is how I came to view myself as my career unfolded at HP.

There were other things going on at home with Pam that also defined who I was as I moved from a recent college graduate into a young adult about to become a father. I was in love and extremely grateful for the good fortune that had led me to be Pam's husband living in Boise. The component of who I was to become as my career advanced and my family grew was now on a defined arc, and that was just fine with me.

When Pam died, I was left fundamentally unbalanced. The most influential person in my life was gone, and I was adrift amidst grief, confusion, and deep sadness. Working with my grief counselor enabled me to start to address some of this, but the question of why I was still here was for me to figure out. The most obvious answer was that I was the remaining parent of Geoff and Jessica, and I needed to take that role seriously. They had just lost their mom, and I was going to do all I could to ensure that they knew that I was supporting them. I had four grandchildren (they call me "J-Paa"), and they had slightly different needs since they'd just lost Grandma Pam. Family life and its obligations are hardwired deep within me, and I understood what I needed to do. I recognized that I had the chance to impart some tribal elder wisdom to my children and their wives now and then. But I needed to choose those times carefully and watch out for indulging in this too much or too enthusiastically with these accomplished and very successful young adults.

How was I going to deal with my life going forward, and who was this new guy going to be? That's where my training at HP and my default of being a goal-driven person kicked into gear. And this is where I hope this book might occupy a unique niche in the journals of grief and personal growth. I knew I needed to define my intent going forward. My early days of grief told me that this process was not going to be hurried by my intentions. I needed to sit down and lay out the problem as I saw it and then sit down for a lot longer to give my heart time to catch up with my cognition.

There were a couple of issues: I needed to figure out a way to accept that Pam was gone, and I needed to make good decisions about who the new John was going to be. The acceptance piece continues to be a significant challenge. I believe this will be a long-term process, and I'm not fully clear on what acceptance will look or feel like. But I'm committed to supporting forward progress in whatever forms it might take. My reinvention is a lot simpler and probably more aligned with that left-brain orientation that has defined me for so long. Life is finite. There are significant issues in the United States. Being kind to myself and to everyone I encountered was a very good starting point for defining the new John. And continuing to look for and actively pursue ways to leave it better than I found it fits this intention well.

These plans could not be solely head-driven; they needed to very fundamentally involve my heart as well. They needed to acknowledge what I'd learned so far about how I processed my grief. It didn't look or feel like anything that I'd ever done in the past. My journey proceeds at its own pace, and my head *and* heart must be equally involved in making progress.

From my time in Rotary Youth Exchange and as board chairman of Semilla Nueva, I learned that I have some leadership chops. I can see the bigger picture better now. I worked for a lot of terrific managers at HP, and I noted many of the tactics and skills that made them good at that job. I was never one to invent the wheel or pioneer new interpersonal skills. I was good at recognizing excellence and then applying my skills and brainpower to further optimize what was already known. I also recognized that my heartbroken status had started a process of making me a better listener and a more empathetic human. These skills also fed into the model of effective leadership.

My time in Rotary Youth Exchange also showed me that I had a voice that could be used effectively in mentoring. This was part of my decision to lead Boise Sunrise. I had numerous opportunities to interface with students through various service projects through Rotary. In addition to giving out dictionaries to third graders, I used these opportunities to shamelessly advocate for reading and literacy. The club had several projects aimed at advocacy for youth (STEM education, housing, more book projects, and our ongoing support of all manner of projects at Hope House in Marsing, Idaho), and I naturally gravitated to these. I chose my words carefully, but they always included an assertion that we *saw* these students and sought to support and benefit them in what we believed was an effective way.

And I think I can influence my friends and colleagues with my demeanor. Right after Pam died, my default was to simply go quiet because I didn't know what to say, and my mind was still so thoroughly confused by just about everything around me. I began to emerge from this self-imposed silence about six months after Pam's death. I'd already decided on a couple of things about the future John. One was to pay closer attention to both my head *and* my heart. As I moved through my grief, I got clues about what might be next or what might be a good idea if I took the time to notice and acknowledge things and events around me—to simply pay attention. I've already talked about wanting to be a better listener. I had a *lot* of room for growth here, and I intuitively knew that if I listened better, everyone would benefit. Finally, I wanted to re-embrace what I thought was a decent sense of humor. When I combined these three, I thought I could be an enjoyable and entertaining conversation partner. And as I experienced coffee chats with friends, it seemed that humor could brighten their day. I wanted to demonstrate that I was a resilient individual who would rise strong from the blow of losing Pam.

And now, I want to share what I've learned as a means of serving others. Initially, I put a focus on connecting with men in grief, especially American men, because there are numerous cultural details at work as we process deep loss and grief in this country. My experience is that addressing grief and death is avoided in our culture. My quiet phone after Pam's death was proof of this. I don't think my friends recognized that I needed empathy and compassion until I asked for these things. I had a circle of high-character friends, but my being in need was a new and unfamiliar status to them. Until I shone a bright light on how damaged I was from losing my wife, I don't think it registered on their radar. The consistency of this experience told me that our cultural avoidance of death and grief is a statement about where we are collectively, as opposed to an accurate descriptor of these friends as individuals.

Thus, I've expanded that target to include *all* of us who are strivers, problem solvers, and left-brain-leaning individuals, regardless of gender. My training in college and in my professional career offered nothing that positioned me to effectively understand the emotional and psychological aspects of grief. I got a little of this from my involvement in faith communities along the way, but I was not at all prepared for what I had to address after Pam died. My experience in the faith-based Grief

Share was that they wanted to help, but they had their own program that I needed to embrace. Parts of that worked for me and others were not aligned with where I was and where I thought I needed to go next. I was in way over my head, and I knew it. The most positive and impactful actions I took were to ask for help, do a lot of reading, and candidly acknowledge who I really was as a left-brain geek. When I accepted my left-brain nature, I could see that I had to develop new skills and learn new things if I was to be successful in addressing this deep grief. Empathy, compassion, kindness, and truly embracing uncomfortable feelings were examples of the new right-brain skills I'd need to develop to move forward.

Another reason why I'm still here is because I seek *to leave positive ripples in my wake*. This purpose came to me as I examined all the intense angst and anger in the US right now. We are deeply divided ideologically, and we are deeply frustrated at what a mutating virus can do to our relatively well-ordered lives. There's damage everywhere you look, and I hoped to be able to do something about that with my chosen behaviors.

But there was more to this story. I wanted to improve people's lives and attitudes whenever I could, so I started thinking about how I might achieve that goal. There are many ways to do this, but I'll share just a few. When we were all locked down during the pandemic, I did a lot of my shopping online. This allowed me to stay home, and products would appear on my doorstep. At my son's house, I noticed a shoebox by his front door that was filled with small bags of chips, candy bars, and bottles of water. A note of sincere appreciation to the delivery drivers from FedEx, UPS, Amazon, and USPS for their efforts was also prominently displayed on the box. I went home and filled up my own box and placed it on my front porch the next day.

Another aspect of COVID isolation was how much business was done by phone. At its most basic description, these folks on the phone were solving some problem *for me.* I always strove to be patient and to verbally deliver a sincere thank you to them for their efforts on my behalf. But I saved one last line for the end of the call. Once our business was done, I asked them to please take the rest of the day off. This would always trigger a laugh. If it was an especially deep laugh, I would veer into self-deprecating mode and embellish that request by asking them to tell their boss that I knew it was a lot for them to have to deal with me. I added that this was the least I could do to express my appreciation for their hard work. Those phone calls would always end on a high note. Mission accomplished; positive ripple left in my wake.

Finally, I strive to choose the right moment to say a sincere thank you. Adding something along the lines of, "I appreciate all your hard work, and I hope your day is a good one," is a terrific way to cement that message of gratitude. This kind of messaging can be in person, online, or in any interaction you have.

I'm developing a park in Boise to highlight Rotary's pillars of service in the areas of peace and environmental sustainability. This story took an interesting turn after the summer of 2020. The first project was to plant the desired vegetation in a wetland area next to the Boise River. This is an eighteen-acre parcel near Willow Lane. The lead for the project explained that the City of Boise was open to partnering with Rotary in a light-footprint development model. We could remove invasive species and plant the right kinds of plants. The city had no money to devote to this project but would partner with us to complete the design and development. A theme of honoring peace and habitat restoration was already in place. When I became involved, the big question was how and where to obtain the funding.

A few weeks after that initial planting project, I experienced a revelation of startling clarity. We do not get a lot of these in our lives, but this was one of them. *I was going to be the funder for the project, and it was going to honor Pam.* There was no question in my mind that this was the right thing to do. Our development model would have crushed gravel paths and peace poles along the paths. We would deploy benches throughout the area, and it would carry the name Wetland Peace Preserve. There would be handsome entrance areas and related signage. The rest of the area would remain unchanged and allow the beauty of a natural wetland to be preserved right in the middle of town.

At the time of this writing, the project design is almost complete. Development and building will hopefully start within months. That park is one of the reasons that I'm still here. I believe this is going to be an extremely handsome park, and I'm comforted by the fact that it will be here long after I am gone.

I'm still here for several reasons. It took me a while to figure this out, but I feel the gentle nudge of the Hand of Providence. I'm taking up space, and I'm using resources on this planet. Part of me says that I need to justify this. But a much more positive part of me tells me to recognize what I do well and to use those skills to leave it better than I found it as often as I can. That is what reaching for a goal just beyond my current grasp looks like at this point in my life.

I will never be the same guy I was when Pam was alive. But in the solitude and the quiet of my house, I have the space and the time to figure out what can be next for me. This life is meant to be lived. Finding and following your path is a worthy use of your time and talents.

MOVING FORWARD
IN THIS NEW LIFE

When I started writing this book, I wanted to deliver something valuable to readers who took the time to read about what I'd learned. Writing also allowed me to take a step back and view individual lessons learned, as well as take stock of the new person I was becoming. This, in and of itself, was healing.

The feedback I received from close friends was that I might have a new point of view on grief. The journey through grief was certainly new to me. In retrospect, I'd led a fairly sheltered life when it came to tragedy, untimely death, or out-of-sequence departures. I was a true neophyte in this space, borderline clueless. Losing the love of my life changed all of that in a dramatic way, and I'm glad I asked for help early on because I had no context or prior experience in dealing with something of this magnitude. But the fact that I had so much to learn and that I had kind friends who were helping me where and when they could allowed me to embrace gratitude while I inched forward.

Grief will touch all of us. There are many flavors and magnitudes of this component of life. As Americans, I don't think we deal with death very well, which seems to be a cultural norm more than a personal characteristic. Death is viewed as the enemy and something to be avoided or resisted at all costs. But it's part of the agreement we make in living this life. It will come to all of us eventually, and it will invade the lives of a vast majority of us when a loved one dies. This calls for us to engage death on terms that we can understand. Ignoring loss and grief is not an effective approach.

Death will almost certainly test our faith in some way. What happens after we die is a mystery, so a theological component will probably be involved for many of us. There are other forms of faith that will also be tested if/when we find ourselves left behind by the death of a loved one. There's always the question, "What am I supposed to do *now*?"

Living through the death of a loved one reminds us of the finite nature of our lives. This life *will end*. What shall we do with the gift that we now hold in our hands? While we have unavoidable obligations that we must attend to in our lives, the bigger picture allows us to see our life as a set of opportunities. We will build a legacy of some sort while we're alive, and we get to influence these decisions if we make the time to think them through and decide. Choosing well is a big deal.

Maintaining our health moves to the top of the list quickly if we're honest with ourselves. If our health declines, our overall quality of life suffers. I learned this lesson as I was battling cancer in 2012 and 2013. What we eat, how we move, how much we sleep, how we manage stress, and how we relate to others are direct components of our physical health that we can substantially influence.

I came to a space where I was no longer afraid of dying, but thoughts of my mortality took a different shape when I pondered what my future might be like if I was stricken with a chronic illness or disability. I have the power to delay decline by prioritizing lifestyle choices.

Living in the moment and embracing gratitude did a lot to calm my emotionally overwrought mind and heart. I couldn't change the past, and per the Serenity Prayer, I needed to find a way to accept the things I could not change. My future was unknown, but I was committed to a healthier lifestyle and paying attention to what was around me. I strove to embrace the future, and my mantra became *be right here, right now*. When I added gratitude to this fully present mindset, I believed I was doing all I could to live this life to the best of my ability. This is how I move forward these days, and I believe it has served me well. I do a lot of planning that enables me to meet stated goals and enjoy chosen experiences. My head is in the moment, my eyes are facing forward, and my heart is open to what is in my life now.

I still have a long path ahead in managing grief. I know that acceptance is a big part of the goal, and I understand that I move toward it very slowly. I do *not* get to choose the pace at which this happens. My job is to remain present, pay attention, and have faith that acceptance will eventually come to pass. I still miss Pam every day, but I'm frequently reminded that there are many others on this path of managing deep grief. When I get a chance to talk to another widow or widower, I always walk away with my heart lightened. I know that I've communicated with someone who knows the magnitude of this pain, and I almost always learn something new from these encounters.

Thus, I offer a list of ways to wrestle with and understand your own method of grieving after a significant loss.

- Seek a qualified grief counselor and talk about how you are feeling.
- Consider joining a grief support group. You'll hear some things that resonate with you and others that don't. Most importantly, you'll meet others who are in the same position. That will feed you as they *get it*— unlike all the others who have not experienced this kind of disaster.
- Keep reading. The books I mentioned helped put me back together. There are important concepts in these books that I simply didn't know. I didn't agree with everything, but I found specific nuggets that worked for me, and that was a big deal.
- Embrace the fact that you'll never be the same again— and realize that you can now choose who that new person will be. That empowerment and feeling of control over something in life was a major milestone for me. I didn't get a vote in Pam's death. But I got the only vote in the details of who the new John would be.
- Consider volunteer opportunities. You get to meet terrific people when you put yourself in play like this. And service, at least for me, was a very effective healing balm for my broken heart.

If I had the choice, I would never have chosen this path. Alas, that's not how it works. I now have the chance to be a role model. I lost the one person on Earth who truly knew me, and this hurts deeply. I'm not the only one who's been forced to take this journey. I wish to actively grieve well in the hope that it helps others. I seek to demonstrate resilience and honor my departed wife by living a life of substance that would make her proud.

I will never forget Pam. She formed many aspects of the person I am, and I truly was part of a great love as her husband.

Now I need to decide what's next and be open to learning a lot of things that I wish I'd learned earlier in my life. My right brain is indeed awakening. Grief has taught me many things about the life that I now choose to embrace, and I wish the same for you.

FINDING LOVE AGAIN

To love again—this is a topic that I've sat with a lot since I decided to write these chapters. How do I tell this story? How do I honor Pam? How do I proceed in exploring a new romantic relationship after losing my wife of thirty-nine years? There may be a cultural norm regarding a waiting period before dating, but I followed my heart. These aren't easy questions, and I believe I only have partial answers to share, but I'll strive to be candid.

I felt I was part of a power couple when Pam and I were married. We had a visibly warm relationship. I never thought much about it, but we were always comfortable in each other's company, and there was rarely annoyance or chilliness between us. We were in love and not hesitant to show our affection as a normal part of our shared demeanor.

After Pam died, I heard more than once that others had greatly admired what we had and had wanted to emulate this type of romantic relationship. This was somewhat soothing to hear, but it was also slightly foreign and challenging as I was grieving the loss of my true love. Then I wondered if I would ever get a chance at something like this again.

I began dating in 2020 because I was lonely. I felt I had something to offer, and I wanted to see if I could handle being in the dating market. I realized that the way my father had raised me created a deep respect for women. I was not allowed to use the pronoun "she" when referring to my mom. If I did when Dad was within earshot, he would be right in my grill, stressing that I must refer to her as "Mom." I got the message.

My self-esteem was at rock bottom after Pam died. I hadn't been able to stop the progression of the cancer, even though I embraced the various tasks of being her caregiver. But essentially, I was an observer, as this unstoppable force slowly took her from me in the fall of 2019. I felt a tangible component of failure in all of this and wondered if anyone would find me attractive or interesting.

Thus started "the education of John" in terms of relating to the opposite sex in a way that I hadn't embraced for over forty-five years. I consciously chose to improve my listening skills. I had a vision of what a gentleman behaved like, and I wanted to be that guy. I paid attention to what I felt and how I perceived being perceived as I inched forward in this new space. I wanted to be wanted. I guess my initial goal (you can now see how much of my conscious life was built around driving toward known *goals*) was that I wanted to reconnect with love in this new life.

So, I dipped my toe in the water with online dating. This was a strange new world, and I proceeded carefully in terms of striving to be a gentleman. I had no idea if I would be attractive to women, but I remained hopeful. One relationship started, and I was surprised at how quickly it heated up into intimacy. I didn't know what I didn't know, but I strove to keep my eyes open and to be honest with myself about the feelings I now experienced. I'll always be grateful for that relationship in terms of the compassion I felt from that romantic partner and how she helped me to start feeling again—as well as to rebuild my self-esteem. I felt twinges of guilt from time to time, but I came to accept my feelings. I believed that Pam would have wanted me to seek happiness again. That relationship ended a few months after it started, but I was glad I could experience romantic feelings again.

I met Janice in 2020. I immediately felt care and support from her, and I could see that she was an excellent listener. Now I had a role model for what good listening skills looked like. This time, I took the relationship much slower. One of my first epiphanies was that I could candidly talk about my feelings and about Pam without drama or negative vibes from Janice. The more I thought about this when we were apart, the more astounding I found this to be. And I continue to be amazed about this aspect of our friendship that continues to the present day. If a romantic partner was intolerant of me thinking about and talking about my departed wife, it would be a deal breaker.

I observed that one model of dating after loss could manifest itself as transferring feelings for a lost spouse to a new potential partner. A new and attractive potential partner is discovered, and the love that had been directed toward the deceased spouse is now transferred to this new love interest. I'm not sure how common this is, but I suspect that it occurs on a regular basis and that it represents an effective healing model for many widowers. I say this with no judgment. If it works for someone, then that makes it worth pursuing, although I occasionally wonder if the necessary grieving can occur in these cases.

This was *never* going to be the path I chose to walk. I deeply felt the need to wrestle with the pain of Pam's death directly and openly and to find a way to accept that awful event that I couldn't change. I had work to do in actively engaging my grief, and that involved a good share of looking inward and backward.

I found that I was desperately lonely. Inherent in this was that I didn't fare well alone. I wanted to move forward, and I wanted someone to share life with. I wanted a companion. I also wanted someone who wanted me. I wondered how many women out there could love all the facets of me. I knew I was suffering and was a complicated puzzle, and loving me would be a challenge for anyone. I was a neophyte in dating, as I had lost my heart to Pam at a young age. I had a lot that I needed to learn, and I needed to honor my head and my heart as I moved forward in any romantic relationship. Furthermore, I didn't want to leave any interpersonal damage in my wake, so I needed to proceed carefully and choose my words and actions with all of this in mind.

Next, I had to understand the details of what attracted me. I wanted a physically fit and compassionate woman who liked me a lot. Janice checked those boxes. I was more than a little stunned when old friends pointed out her resemblance to Pam. I learned a lot from Janice because her path had included a career as a hospice nurse and learning about grief in addition to studying depth psychology. She was intelligent, communicated very well, and was interested in areas of life that I knew little about. When I shared my areas of interest and talked about the changes I was trying to manage in my life, she was a terrific listener. It took me many weeks to be able to step back and see this new relationship in an objective manner, but when I did, I concluded that Pam and Janice would have been fast friends. This was a valuable insight, and it came with a tangible component of mental comfort for me. I began to see the time with Janice as a true respite from grief work. I could strive to be my authentic self (I was learning who that was, albeit slowly) and where I could position myself for healing. We were sounding boards for each other, and this was valuable and intimate time for us to get to know each other better. I've used the phrase "true love" in describing Pam, and I stand by that description. Janice and I carved out a new space and created a "new love" that acknowledged our pasts, which were unique to us. I was a lucky man to be able to experience this. Sharing in a transparent way revealed myself and helped us build a strong, honest relationship.

I found that the rhythm of the relationship was surprisingly important to me. I needed alone time and significant amounts of solitude to engage in this journey of processing my grief. Fortunately, Janice understood this, and it didn't become a major point of contention in our growing relationship. I needed to figure out several things, and many of these required me to lead with my head on my back deck while I was alone.

When I was with Janice, I made the decision to be as fully present as I could. I wanted to be honest and candid, listen well, and be emotionally available to her when we were together. We had togetherness and space in equal measure, which we worked out between us.

I was amazed that someone as extraordinary as Janice was not already in a committed relationship. How was she still on the market? Then I would embrace gratitude by realizing that I was the one who she came to love.

I wanted to ensure that all I did to move forward represented my desire to honor Pam. Being in a relationship with Janice was something that never felt dishonorable, and I'm grateful it wasn't a major impediment for me to overcome. This was to be the start of the rest of my life. I wanted to do it well and on my terms. Finding Janice was a big-time good fortune that landed in my lap. I didn't want to screw this up as I slowly learned how I wanted to proceed with this new life. I wanted to do right by her while simultaneously allowing myself time to grieve. I slowly learned how to do this over the course of 2020 and 2021—amidst the madness of a global pandemic.

One of the more interesting decisions I had to make was how and when to introduce Janice to my children and friends. I sat with this one for a while, as there were many ways I could accomplish this. I could mention her in a Facebook post. I could introduce her when we were out and about meeting friends in an opportunistic manner. I could invite her to a Rotary meeting or a dinner party. I took this slow, and I thought a lot about what I was going to say and how I wanted these introductions to proceed. Friends were generally happy for me to be romantically involved. I was especially careful with my children and my grandchildren, and in the end, these introductions went very well. I'm glad I didn't wing it with my circle of loved ones. These events needed to be approached with care and forethought. I was more than a little nervous but ultimately grateful that this all happened in a smooth and benefit-of-the-doubt manner. Everyone gets along; this is no surprise, given the kind of person Janice is.

I will never and can never forget my wife. Pam was a major influence on the man that I am. I wrestled with how to honor her and how to also acknowledge my desire to be in a relationship again. This is a touchy subject, especially within the frame of American culture. How long was I supposed to wait until I could consider a new romantic partner? How was I to behave to be that gentleman I wished to be? What was the right path for me?

It's important for me to acknowledge significant dates and anniversaries. These include Pam's birth and death dates, our wedding anniversary, and the number of months since she passed away. I always shared the emotional impact of these with Janice, and she freely and empathetically gave me support. Yes, it's possible to simultaneously deepen a dating relationship and grieve. This is important. If you're dating someone who thinks you should completely forget your deceased spouse and be finished grieving, this person does *not* understand you or your emotions. Love is integrated into one's very being.

I experienced extremely good fortune in meeting and loving Janice. My life continues with a high-character, intelligent, compassionate, and adventurous woman by my side. I experienced good luck, and I also *made* my share of good luck in these last few years. If losing the love of your life is what you are currently grieving, I wish this kind of good fortune for you. It can happen. There is life to be lived, and if you are like me, you live better with a committed companion at your side.

EPILOGUE – NUGGETS OF WISDOM

The variety of my days as a widower is sometimes worth pondering, as it is now more than two years since I lost Pam. There are days when things go well, and I feel like I'm back in the groove of living my life. Those days are typically filled with worthy distractions, and thus, I find myself not thinking much about Pam. There are other days, often associated with a quiet house, when my thoughts turn to her more frequently. I feel a fifty-ton weight on my chest, and I know I cannot remove it. I can manage it with various techniques, but it remains steadfast.

In my more contemplative moments, I recognize where I am now versus where I was shortly after her death. And I think of that phrase, *"What doesn't kill you makes you stronger."* No, this whole experience hasn't killed me and has made me stronger. I know, I know. That turn of a phrase is not helpful to the reader and can leave you wondering if I know what I'm talking about at all. But I'm confident that it's accurate because I have directly experienced it a number of times. I'm still here.

I've developed some interesting new patterns since Pam departed. I set the alarm for 5:00 a.m. on the local NPR station. I listen to the earliest version of Morning Edition as I lie at somewhat less than 100 percent awake. It's always interesting to see how much I've absorbed and how much I've missed when I listen again later in the morning as I'm eating breakfast. I bet Pam wouldn't be thrilled with this new habit if she was in bed with me. It's a manifestation of the freedom I now have that allows me to continue this odd new practice. I value my mornings and am usually at my best when the world and my hometown are quiet and generally asleep.

As I considered the damaged status of our American culture, I saw it with slightly new eyes and made some decisions about my behaviors. My primary intention is my desire to be *kind*. This started as an intention to be kind to myself, and it quickly morphed into something that I wanted to demonstrate to everyone. This is the kind of role model I want to be. I also want to give everyone the benefit of the doubt, listen as well as I can, and hold my opinions a little closer to my chest as a component of listening better. There was a *lot* of room for improvement in these spaces. I sought to prioritize my abilities to *understand* others and lifted off the gas a little on my desire to *be understood*. I want to express gratitude with frequent utterances of "Thank you" to everyone I meet.

I always find it interesting and instructional when I can see the right side of my brain at work. Before, my levels of empathy were low until I was knocked down by achieving sobriety, then defeating cancer, and now confronting deep grief. I occasionally feel embarrassed as I think about the unfeeling person I used to be. I'm glad this is changing, but it seems to be a process that's aligned with paying attention rather than any intent that I might assign to it. It goes right along with that listening goal. Truly hearing what is bothering someone else and then seeking to be empathetic is a satisfying evolution for me to analyze. I'm glad it's happening. Knowing what I know now, I wish I'd started the process earlier. But I need to own my past and use it to instruct my chosen future. I have a long way to go in being the kind of effective and natural empath that I see in so many other people. But I've embarked on the journey, and this transformation is a fundamental part of healing from the blow of becoming a widower.

Grief is all around me, and I wish to demonstrate resilience as I move forward after Pam's death. I have a strong intent not to be a victim.

I wish to reference a poem by Ralph Waldo Emerson:

This Is My Wish For You

This is my wish for you:
Comfort on difficult days
Smiles when sadness intrudes
Rainbows to follow the clouds
Laughter to kiss your lips
Sunsets to warm your heart
Hugs when spirits sag
Beauty for your eyes to see
Friendships to brighten your being
Faith so that you can believe
Confidence for when you doubt
Courage to know yourself
Patience to accept the truth
Love to complete your life

In no particular order, these are my nuggets of wisdom—how I learned to get into my grief:

- Recognize that *pain* cannot be avoided and is best addressed with a direct look and a welcoming attitude.

It's here. Set out a chair for it. See it clearly and speak to it directly. Shouting and screaming are allowed as you address this new and unwanted companion in your life.

- Be present with your feelings and thoughts. Feel them. Try to understand them. Realize that understanding is likely to take a while, but commit to being present to these less-than-pleasant feelings that are in your emotional basket.

- When intense emotions ambush you, think about responding in a particular manner. Push back. Confront those intense feelings with an intent of your own. "What are you, and why are you here now?" Strive to name those nasty feelings and give yourself time to sit with them and understand them to the best of your ability. Tell those painful feelings that you see them and that they will not be ignored. Set an intent to dissect them along the lines of how they made you feel, when they showed up, and maybe a little deductive logic to figure out why they appeared when they did. And if other things in your life demand your attention, tell these intense feelings that you will be back to deal with them later.

- Keep reading. I have mentioned multiple books, and they are listed in the Appendix. There are a lot of terrific writers out there. Be ready to cherry-pick some of their best ideas if they seem to describe some of your feelings and challenges. That's what I did. I learned a lot with my reading, but I didn't accept or internalize all the feedback that came from these books. Grab the concepts that work for you and leave the rest.

- Realize that the old you will change, given the disaster that has caused all this grief. Then take some time to think about who you want that new person to be.

This is incredibly empowering. *You get to decide aspects of your future.* There are things you cannot change (remember the Serenity Prayer), but your future does not fall into that category. You're still here for a reason. It's primarily up to you to figure that out and to influence who that new person will be.

- Give yourself time and strive to remain confident that progress can be made if you pay attention to your feelings and thoughts. That progress, for me, was incredibly slow. But I can see how much different I am now when compared to that heartbroken and befuddled new widower in late 2019. Believe in yourself.

- Seek gratitude whenever you can. That can be backward-looking in terms of how fortunate you were to have had the now-missing person in your life. There are many blessings that we enjoy as Americans. We just need to look for them. Seeing them and appreciating them is not dishonoring your grief. In the spirit of now looking forward, gratitude gives you some excellent building blocks to start putting yourself back together. Recognizing blessings with honest gratitude is a positive and powerful force that can guide you into your chosen future.

- Don't bury your grief. And realize that there will be a nudge from American culture to do this. This hurts. But it's widely agreed that actively addressing your grief is how to figure out the way forward. I desperately miss Pam. But I'm still here, and I don't want to be a placeholder until I see her again. Buried grief will find a way to bite you when you aren't looking. In fact, I have found that well-addressed grief can also deliver that painful bite. But by wrestling with it directly, you position yourself to find your path forward. You will develop your own effective coping tactics.

- Be careful with alcohol and other inebriants. While they can temporarily dull the pain you feel, they can become a crutch and an inhibitor to the soul-searching work that needs to be done.
- You will find a way to put grief deep into your bones. It will be with you the rest of your days, but it's manageable if you look right at it. Deep grief becomes a significant component of your story. That is truth. It can be carried, and a new life can be configured. Don't ignore or bury your unaddressed grief.
- Look at the formative influences in your life with your new eyes. These include faith, God, and church. They also encompass family and friends. How did these areas give you strength and comfort in your journey with grief? These are not simple answers, and they aren't answers that I can provide you. They need to be sorted out by you, acknowledging all that has happened since your life was blown up by the loss of your loved one.
- Grief can be viewed as a puzzle. I believe that everyone's puzzle is unique to them. I've shared some of the pieces of my puzzle in the hopes that some of them might work for you as well.

I will always love Pam. She is part of who I am, and I was part of a great love as her husband. Now with her passing, my right brain is, indeed, awakening, and grief has taught me many things about life that I now choose to embrace. I wish the same for you.

APPENDIX – RECOMMENDED READING

Brené Brown, *Rising Strong: How the Ability to Reset Transforms the Way We Live, Love, Parent, and Lead*

Megan Devine, *It's OK That You're Not OK: Meeting Grief and Loss in a Culture That Doesn't Understand*

Kathleen Dowling Singh, *The Grace in Dying*

Jill Bolte Taylor, Ph.D., *My Stroke of Insight: A Brain Scientist's Personal Journey*

Tom Zuba, *Permission to Mourn: A New Way to Do Grief*

Tom Zuba, *Becoming Radiant: A New Way to Do Life Following the Death of a Beloved.*

ACKNOWLEDGMENTS

This book would not have been possible without the support of critical and empathetic individuals in my life. Janice Ehrhart tops that list, and I wish to thank her for her belief in me, for her efforts to understand and love me, and for her excellent editing skills. Next on that list is my grief counselor, Jerri Walker. Jerri opened my eyes and my heart to effective ways of dealing with grief that hit me like a tidal wave. I wish to thank Geoff and Jessica for their support as I engaged in this journey. They lost their mother and have had their own journeys of grief to navigate along with their spouses and children.

I wish to acknowledge all my sisters and brothers at the Rotary Club of Boise Sunrise and my friends all around District 5400. You saw me and listened to me and dealt with me with care and true compassion. To my friend Steve Banick, I wish to offer a special thanks because he encouraged me to engage this writing project and identified the niche that I hope this book can fill. To my editor Nancy Erickson, I thank you for your patience and skills in helping to make this book more readable without losing my voice along the way.

To everyone out there who obtains this book and reads it, I wish you well on your journey through grief. There is hard work involved here, and I hope the book gives you some ideas on how to engage that work and begin the process of assembling your life after the loss of your loved one. Be well.

ABOUT THE AUTHOR

J ohn Lodal lives in Boise, Idaho. He's a retired development engineer who worked for Hewlett Packard for thirty-two years. He holds three patents and a fistful of pleasant memories of a productive, instructive, and enjoyable career.

John plays trombone in a jazz big band and bass guitar for whoever asks him to sit in. He is a Rotarian and a member of the board of directors of the non-profit Semilla Nueva. Service to his hometown and to the world at large is a big deal to this self-avowed impact junkie. He's constantly motivated to leave it better than he found it.

John has two children and four grandchildren. He enjoys the outdoor lifestyle afforded by living in Southwest Idaho, and he enjoys traveling to new places.

As part of a series of videos that my counselor filmed and posted during the COVID pandemic, she interviewed me in March 2021. As you might guess, we spoke of grief. These were called "Mental Health Mondays" and were posted on YouTube. You can find it here: https://tinyurl.com/johnlodal. You can also find this video if you search for "*YouTube Mental Health Mondays John Lodal*."

CPSIA information can be obtained
at www.ICGtesting.com
Printed in the USA
BVHW080258021222
653210BV00003B/19

9 781955 711203